THE INFLUENCE MINDSET

THE ART AND SCIENCE OF GETTING PEOPLE TO CHOOSE YOU

CHRISTIAN HANSEN

The Influence Mindset:
The Art And Science Of Getting People To Choose You

Table of Contents

Why Your Message Matters

Let's get right to the point:

Your message is your greatest tool to influence others to choose you. The problem is, most people fail because they don't know how to position and sell themselves. Their message gets lost in the noise.

Because our brains are wired to pay attention to certain things, when you build your message on three key (research-backed) strategies, you will bypass the brain's defenses, stand out from the crowd, and influence Decision Makers to choose you...every single time.

This book tells you how.

This All Started Because
I Fell Off My Bike
(In Front of a Bunch of People)

I was looking forward to my first ride of the season. The weather had finally warmed up, and the day before, I had taken my bike out of storage and began the tedious process of getting it tuned back into shape.

I filled the tires full of air.

I cleaned the chain of months of dust and grime.

I even tightened the seat, tested the brakes, and double-checked my helmet straps.

I was all set.

And so the next morning, I woke up bright and early feeling confident things would go smoothly. Walking out to the street with my bike, I imagined how it would feel to once again fly down the bike path and feel the wind whipping around me. I envisioned cutting around the sharp corners and testing my speed on the straightaways. Noticing my neighbors enjoying their morning walks, I cheerfully waved as I swung my leg around, mounted the seat, and pressed my feet to the pedals.

Filled with anticipation and with my bike ready to go, I pushed off and began pedaling towards the sunrise.

Except for one problem.

Instead of the rhythmic click and whirl of the wheels propelling me forward, I heard the worst sound a biker can ever hear: the rasping wheeze of chain being raked across metal.

My bike chain had somehow disconnected from the gears, and my dreams of a smooth ride were fading fast.

However, still having the momentum of my initial launch, I frantically pedaled (hoping against hope) that something would click. But as precious seconds ticked away, it was clear that I was doomed. With my feet locked in and furiously pumping, my bike began to wobble from side to side. As my neighbors watched frozen in wide-eyed alarm, I collided with a row of trash cans, sending bags, banana peels, and moldy bread flying everywhere.

Thus began (and ended) my first ride of the season.

Hobbling back, with my pride just as bent as my front wheel, I wondered what had happened?

My tires were pumped.

My chain was clean.

My helmet was on. I had done everything right!

The problem was that I had no idea there was a disconnect between the chain and the gears. Even though I was generating power, I wasn't creating movement—which was what I really wanted. And so despite my best efforts and preparation, I crashed.

I later realized that this exact same problem happens to all of us. However, instead of bikes and morning rides, it happens in critical moments where our chances for success hang in the balance. We may be prepared; we may have our tires pumped and helmets ready to go, but sometimes there is a disconnect between our efforts and the results, and we crash.

And we have no idea why.

❝ Sometimes there is a disconnect between our efforts and the results. ❞

Lots of People Spin Their Wheels, but Few Move Forward

Throughout my career I have worked in undergraduate and graduate admissions as well as in corporate HR. As I reviewed and interviewed thousands of candidates, I quickly realized I had a front row seat in learning how people deal with one of the biggest challenges we face in life: How do you stand out when everyone else is trying to stand out too?

Here's what I learned:

Most of our lives, we operate in a world that values and rewards performance.

If you study hard? You get good grades.

If you work hard? You get promoted.

If you deliver quality service? Your clients will come back again and again.

But every once in a while, we face certain "make it or break it" moments like college applications, job interviews, and even pitches to new clients where the doors of opportunity open or close.

If you succeed? New paths in life are opened to you.

If you fail? Then it's back to the drawing board.

What most people don't know is that being successful in these critical hinge points has little to do with proving how well you perform. Rather, success has everything to do with how you influence people to choose you over everyone else.

The problem is that the vast majority of people have no idea that the tables have turned. They have no clue that in this "make it or break it" moment, cultivating influence (and not proving abilities and performance) is what matters most. What they think works suddenly doesn't anymore.

Their tires are pumped.

Their helmets are strapped on.

They are furiously pedaling. They have done everything right!

But as they spin their wheels, they have no idea there is a fundamental disconnect between their efforts and the results they want. Even though they prove they are qualified, and even though they are generating power, they aren't moving forward. I watched as thousands of individuals confidently got on their bikes, pedaled, and crashed time and time again... and they had no idea why.

Their strategies (however successful elsewhere) had now become liabilities. And they were becoming increasingly frustrated, confused, and discouraged.

It's Not About Being Outstanding...

On the other hand, I also witnessed another group of people who didn't crash. No, instead of hobbling away with bent wheels and injured pride, they rode off into the sunrise ready for new opportunities.

What was their secret? How did they succeed when most others failed?

The answer? While everyone else was concerned about being *outstanding*, these masterful communicators were first concerned about *standing out*.

"While everyone else was concerned about being *outstanding*, these masterful communicators were first concerned about *standing out*."

True, their tires were pumped.

Yes, their helmets were also on.

And, of course, they were pedaling just as hard.

But first and foremost, they had a personal brand message that was designed to stand out when everyone else was trying to stand out too. They were prepared to generate results. But how? How can you make a personal brand message that is designed to rise above the noise and stand out from the crowd?

The problem is this: When your personal brand message is focused on proving you can perform (just like everyone else), and you show how smart, capable, qualified, and passionate you are (also, just like everyone else), your message becomes noise. And it turns out the brain is designed to ignore noise.

However, the brain is also wired to pay attention to certain things. And with a little help from the basic principles of neuroscience, you can learn the fundamentals of how to craft a personal brand message that is designed to bypass the brain's defenses and stand out every single time.

At the end of the day, your personal brand message either influences people to say "yes" or it doesn't. It either persuades people to choose you or it doesn't. In today's increasingly competitive world, your success rises or falls on your ability to nudge people to choose you. Your personal brand's influential power is more critical than ever before.

It's Like Riding a Bike

"But wait a second!" you might say, "I'm not sure I even have a specific 'personal brand message' to share."

Or, "I have a direction" you might add, "but I'm not sure where to start or how to give my personal brand a more competitive edge."

Even if you aren't sure what your message is, or even if you don't know where to start; even if your success depends on influencing someone else to choose you over others...this book is for you. Because the amazing thing is that the ability to create influence isn't reserved for a select few that are "born that way." No, after years of studying thousands and thousands of successful communicators, I've discovered that the ability to create influence is something that anyone can learn, practice, and improve.

Just like riding a bike.

Which is what we are going to do together in this book.

Relying on firsthand experiences, stories, and (approachable!) neuroscience research, we will learn the secrets of how to capture attention, establish credibility, and cultivate influence so you can stand out when everyone else is trying to stand out too.

Together we are going to break down the fundamental challenges we face and equip you (step by step) with the tools and perspectives you need to position yourself for success. Plus, because this topic is so important and everyone learns differently, at the end of each chapter I've also provided access to extensive bonus material to help you learn the secrets of personal brand positioning and refining your message. There you can get access to training, resources, and additional advanced content *not* found in the book. Best of all, access to the site is 100% free. Simply go to **(TheChristianHansen.com/BookBonus)** to get started!

Imagine What it Would be Like...

Imagine what it would be like to feel confident knowing that your personal brand message is designed to stand out.

Imagine, that while everyone else is spinning their wheels and crashing, what it would be like to enter a "make it or break it" moment and feel assured your personal brand was engineered to generate results.

More importantly, imagine if you could stand out from the crowd, rise above the noise, and ride off into the sunrise ready to capitalize on the opportunities before you.

Welcome to the Influence Mindset.

SECTION 1:

SMART, CAPABLE, QUALIFIED, AND PASSIONATE

Why Should They Choose You?

"You have to stand out if you want to move up."
—Tom Peters

"**W**hy should they choose you?"

The classroom full of first-year MBA students stared back, each surprised by my unexpected question. I was leading a seminar on "How to Stand Out to Job Recruiters," and a minute before had asked what companies these students were interested in. One by one, each student had raised their hands and confidently listed companies that ranged from major firms that dominate the traditional MBA recruiting cycle to smaller companies that were growing in fast-paced industries.

But with my question, the enthusiastic classroom had turned to a thoughtful pause. In the awkward silence, I raised the question again. "No, seriously. If I was a recruiter meeting you for the first time, why should I choose you over everyone else?"

Whether they were embarrassed to boast in front of their classmates or had never considered the question, the room remained uncomfortably silent. The overhead projector buzzed in the background.

To my left, a student slowly raised his arm. I turned and smiled. "Yes? What would you say?"

"Well," he stammered, "I have three years of experience in finance, which is what I want to do..."

"Impressive!" I encouraged.

He relaxed a bit and continued, "I completed an internship and also majored in finance in my undergrad."

"Anything else you would want to mention?"

"Well, I have a competitive GPA from a highly ranked undergrad program, did really well on my GMAT, and I'm really passionate about numbers and finance in general."

"Excellent," I said. I turned to the whiteboard and wrote:

Competitive grades, scores

Previous experience

Prestigious background

Passion

I turned back to the class and asked, "Anyone else? Why should your target company choose you?"

Another hand went up from the other side of the room; this time from a capable-looking female student. "I worked in the same industry as my target company for four years, I managed several teams, and have been promoted twice," she said confidently.

"Congratulations. That's an impressive background!"

She continued, "I also graduated magna cum laude from my undergrad and scored in the 80th percentile on the GMAT. And, well, I got into this MBA program which is nationally ranked, didn't I? Overall, I feel I'm really qualified."

"You most certainly are!" I said, and as her teammates quietly gave her supportive high fives for her accomplishments, I turned to the board and added a check mark next to each of the areas she had mentioned:

Competitive grades, scores   ✓

Previous experience   ✓

Prestigious background   ✓

Passion

"And would you consider yourself passionate about the job too?" I asked.

"Definitely," she said. I added a ✓ next to "passion".

"Alright, who's next?" I asked.

Slowly more students raised their hands and rattled off their impressive array of experiences. With each student, I added a check mark next to the items on the board. Every one of the reasons they listed fell into one of the categories, and gradually more and more check marks added up.

After about 10 students, I paused, looked at the board, and asked, "Do you see a pattern here?"

Competitive grades, scores	✓✓✓✓✓✓
Previous experience	✓✓✓✓✓✓✓✓
Prestigious background	✓✓✓✓✓✓✓
Passion	✓✓✓✓✓✓✓✓

"When asked, 'why should I choose you?' All of you instinctively mentioned the same things:

- All of you have solid experience
- All of you are passionate for what you want to do
- And the majority of you have competitive scores from prestigious undergraduate institutions.

"If we boil it down," I continued, "all of you are presenting the exact same message to recruiters: that you are smart, capable, qualified, and passionate. But here's the rub: As I've reviewed and interviewed thousands of candidates, pretty much every other applicant has the same message: that they are also smart, also capable, also qualified, and also passionate.

"So, if your message sounds just like everyone else...how can you really stand out when it matters most?"

But if Everyone Else is Doing it….

The fact is, this problem doesn't just affect MBA students. It affects everyone.

Whether you are:

- A student applying to higher education
- A career seeker looking for your next move
- A CEO trying to nail down the final investor
- And even an entrepreneur trying to land the client of a lifetime

…we all face the same problem. When we try to stand out, our messaging inadvertently sounds just like everyone else most of the time. Stacks of college applications are filled with essays preaching about competitive grades and how well-rounded and passionate students are. Endless amounts of job interviews are recitations of facts and achievements. Email inboxes and social media ads are overflowing with business marketing stuffed with rankings, performance awards, and ratings.

Smart, capable, qualified, and passionate.

Wash, rinse, repeat.

At the end of the day, most people sound just like everyone else. And when your personal brand message merely echoes all of your competition, your message becomes meaningless noise. The result? That noise is ignored, your message fails to influence, and you miss the critical opportunities you desperately want.

The bigger question is, why do we do this? When we know everyone else is saying the same thing, how come we spend so much time trying to breathlessly prove we are smart, capable, qualified, and passionate, just like everyone else?

The reason?

We have been taught to believe that when we effectively prove how well we can perform, we can always reach our goals. In other words, success happens when we apply the Achievement Mindset.

"When your personal brand message merely echoes all of your competition, your message becomes meaningless noise."

CHAPTER 1

The Game Has Changed

"In life, as in football, you won't go far unless
you know where the goalposts are."
—Arnold H. Glasgow

Few things are more entertaining than watching a group of four-year-olds play soccer. My wife and I were enjoying an afternoon in the park one Saturday when we stopped to watch two teams of little tykes duke it out for the biggest game of their lives.

As we watched, two things became abundantly clear:

First, this really wasn't a game with strategies. Rather, it was delightful mayhem. A mob of small, brightly colored jerseys weaved like a flock of sparrows, dispersing and reforming around a ball wherever it went. With little legs furiously kicking every which way, the ball would eventually pop out and roll in another direction, and the shapeless mass of kids would follow.

Second, it was clear there was one feisty little girl who had her wits about her and was driving the ball in a focused direction. She was frequently in the middle of the pack, and whenever the ball shot outwards, she would be the first to reach it and drive it towards the goal. We watched as she scored point after point while the other kids were still dazed and confused about what day it was.

One of the parent referees called halftime, and the kids went to their respective sidelines and refilled with snacks, fruits, and water. Then after a few minutes, faces still pink from exertion, the teams switched sides and started the next half of the game. As before, the ball was mauled from every direction, and again, the same little girl took the lead.

Except for one problem.

This time the little girl didn't grasp the concept that the teams had switched sides. Though she was still dominating the field, she had no idea that she was now scoring on her own goal.

As confusion ensued, coaches and parents from both teams laughed and waved their arms, motioning for her to go in the right direction. The focused little girl didn't notice and continued to cleanly sweep everyone (and everything!) in her path until eventually, the game was paused and one of the parents went out to explain that she needed to focus on the opposite direction instead.

The game resumed and the little girl, clear-eyed and determined, continued to dominate wherever she went.

As we gathered our things and began to walk away, I thought to myself that she was easily the best player on the field, but she had no idea that the game had changed. And effective as her approach was, because she had no idea the game had changed, her strategies achieved (literally) the wrong goal.

When it comes to achieving success, the landscape of the field completely changes sometimes, and therein lies the challenge. Do we realize the shift and adjust our approach? Or do we carry on as before?

As we begin our journey crafting a personal brand that is designed to open the doors of opportunity, we need to first figure out where we are starting from. We need to understand the game we are playing, and why it matters. What are the rules? What determines success?

To do this, we need to briefly define some terms that will provide the foundation for everything we will do from here on out. Specifically, we need to understand three key ideas that will frame our discussion for the rest of the book:

1. The Performance Environment

2. The Achievement Mindset

3. Tribes (and why they are everywhere!)

The more we understand these terms, the more we will be able to avoid common pitfalls that tank most people's chances. Better yet, the more we understand these ideas, the more we will be able to capitalize on hidden opportunities that most people overlook.

The Performance Environment and The Achievement Mindset

Every day of our lives, we live and work in a world that values and rewards performance.

This is not, by any means, a revolutionary idea.

If you work hard in school? You get an A. If you complete your tasks in your job? You get paid. If you provide excellent goods and services in a small business? Customers will return again and again. We have built a world and society that (understandably so) rewards excellent performance. And if you perform well, more and more opportunities are opened to you.

Like I said, this is not rocket science.

Whenever we find ourselves in a situation where performance determines our opportunities, we are in what I call the Performance Environment. For the sake of our discussion, here's how I define it:

THE PERFORMANCE ENVIRONMENT:
Where Success is Based on How Well You Perform

If we live in a world where success is based on how well we perform, we quickly learn how to prove to others that we can perform well. Specifically, we learn to show others that we are smart, capable, qualified, and passionate. This is what I call the Achievement Mindset:

THE ACHIEVEMENT MINDSET:

Belief That Success is Based on Proving You Are Smart, Capable, Qualified, and Passionate

Simply put, in the Performance Environment, the Achievement Mindset is the best strategy for getting ahead. Students who are smart and get good grades are awarded prestigious scholarships. Employees who are capable and qualified are promoted. Entrepreneurs who deliver excellent service profit more and more.

Whether we are in school, work, or running our own businesses, we often find ourselves using the Achievement Mindset in the Performance Environment (because it works!). And because we spend most of our time in situations where performance drives success, we gradually learn to consistently and instinctively apply the Achievement Mindset every chance we get. Hence, we become quite effective and accustomed to proving we are smart, capable, qualified, and passionate.

That is exactly what happened to the MBA students in the previous section. Can you see how their answers all fell within the Achievement Mindset?

(Smart)	→ Competitive grades, scores	✓✓✓✓✓✓
(Capable)	→ Previous experience	✓✓✓✓✓✓✓✓
(Qualified)	→ Prestigious background	✓✓✓✓✓✓✓
(Passionate)	→ Passion	✓✓✓✓✓✓✓✓

In the past when those students wanted to get ahead in school, college, and in their careers, the Achievement Mindset had always done the trick. And so, when they want to stand out to recruiters, why wouldn't they continue to use this reliable and proven approach? Hence the pervasive Achievement Mindset language.

This is the "game" we are playing. This is the "field" we are playing on. These are the "goalposts" we are trying to score in. Every day of our lives, we operate in a world that awards success again and again when we prove to others that we are smart, capable, qualified, and passionate.

Wash, rinse, repeat.

However, the problem that the MBA students didn't know about, and the problem that most of us don't realize, is that the Achievement Mindset works...but only if you are inside *the Tribe.*

The Inside of The Tribe

What do I mean by "the Tribe"?

Anytime there is:

- A group of people
- Who share a common goal
- And share a limited amount of resources

...they are a Tribe. High schools, universities, and businesses are all Tribes because they each have a set amount of people, they share limited resources, and they work towards a common vision and goal. When you are in the Performance Environment, you are *already a part of* the Tribe. And when you are part of the Tribe, the Achievement Mindset works.

Consider these examples:

- In high school and college, since they have budgeted resources for a set number of students, proving you are smart and capable earns you the grade-based scholarships. There are funds allocated for you...because you are part of the Tribe.
- In your company, top performers are valued and rewarded, and so proving you are competent, qualified, and passionate is a reliable strategy to get promoted. You're already on the short list of top contenders...because you are part of their Tribe.

- In your business, repeat clients come back again and again because you are in their trusted network of service providers. They trust and bring their business to you...because they see you as part of their Tribe.

Can you see how we live and operate in a series of "Tribes" for the majority of our lives? Whether it's school, companies, or our business's repeat clients, you are on the "inside". You have earned their trust, proven your value to the group, and are seen as part of "them". Hence, proving you are smart, capable, qualified, and passionate is good enough to continually open the doors of opportunity.

And so, for years we learn and practice how to consistently and effectively perform well. Because in the Performance Environment, that's how you reliably achieve success.

Outside of The Tribe, Looking in

But what if, like the little girl on the soccer team, the goalposts of success suddenly shift, and you have no idea?

What if:

- You are applying to university and are competing against thousands of applicants?
- You are interviewing for a job and are trying to stand out amongst hundreds?
- You are competing for clients in an extremely saturated market?

All of a sudden, you are no longer inside the Tribe trying to move up. Instead you are outside, looking in. And in this predicament, success is no longer based on proving how well you perform. Rather, success is now based on influencing Decision Makers inside of the Tribe to choose you over others. And if the definition of success has changed? All of a sudden proving you are smart, capable, qualified, and passionate no longer brings the results that you want.

❝ What if the goalposts of success suddenly shift and you have no idea? ❞

This is because of one simple fact: Everyone else is using the Achievement Mindset too.

That is exactly the problem the MBA students had (but didn't realize). Just like college applicants applying to universities, professionals trying to win new clients, and entrepreneurs trying to compete in saturated markets, these students didn't understand that they were now on the outside of the Tribe, looking in. Their success was now based on influencing people to choose them and their personal brand messages all sounded exactly the same.

Their strategy had become a liability.

What helps you *get ahead*, doesn't help you *get in*. And if all you know how to do is progress and advance inside the Tribe, you will never influence (and ultimately be invited) from the outside.

The Selective Environment

What a dilemma!

If all our lives we have learned to adapt in the Performance Environment, how can we reach success when we find ourselves in a "make it or break it moment" on the outside of the Tribe? How can we master the skills of getting in, and not just the skills of getting ahead?

The answer?

First, we need to understand this new environment, and more importantly, we need to grasp how Decision Makers think when they have an overwhelming number of candidates to choose from. Because once we know what is really going on behind the scenes, and once we learn how to influence Decision Makers to choose us, we can learn the secrets of how to design a personal brand message that will capture attention and cultivate influence.

The game has changed.

Welcome to the Selective Environment.

Summary

- Most of the time, we operate in groups and relationships that value and reward performance. These groups are called Tribes, and anytime success is based on how well we perform, we are in the Performance Environment.

- Since we live most of our lives in the Performance Environment, we learn to believe that success happens when we prove to others that we are sufficiently smart, capable, qualified, and passionate. This is called the Achievement Mindset.

- The Achievement Mindset works as a way to move up inside of a Tribe, but what happens when you are outside of the Tribe trying to get in?

- Success is no longer based on performance. Rather, success is based on cultivating influence. You are no longer in the Performance Environment. Instead, you are in the Selective Environment.

Bonus

I've created exclusive content to help you apply the principles we cover together. To access them, go to **TheChristianHansen.com/ BookBonus**

Situation:	PERFORMANCE ENVIRONMENT	SELECTIVE ENVIRONMENT
Definition:	Success is based on how well you perform	?
Primary Goal:	Prove you are smart, capable, qualified, and passionate	?
Strategy:	Achievement Mindset	?
?	?	?
?	?	?
?	?	?
?	?	?
?	?	?

CHAPTER 2

How The Brain Blocks Noise (And Your Message Too)

"In a busy marketplace, not standing out is the same as being invisible."
—Seth Godin

One Saturday morning a few years ago, I woke up to every homeowner's nightmare: a persistent dripping noise. Somehow, somewhere, a water pipe was leaking, and I needed to find it fast. I leapt out of bed and soon discovered my worst fear: My kitchen was submerged in several inches of murky brown water.

In a panic, I quickly shut off the water line and built a dam of towels to contain what I called, "Lake Surprise". With the water stopped, I now faced a larger problem: How could I find and fix the broken pipe this early in the morning? I sat at my computer and groggily googled local plumbers.

A quick search showed that there were about 30 plumbers within a 10-mile radius. That's right, 30.

That was way too many!

Overwhelmed by too many choices, I now had a SECOND problem on my hands: How on earth do I choose the right plumber?

Nightmarish stories about shoddy jobs and dishonest plumbers who fleeced people out of thousands of dollars raced through my head. Not only was I worried about the flooded kitchen, but I was ALSO afraid of making the wrong choice! The stakes couldn't have been higher. This was my home; this was a problem I couldn't fix, and I needed help ASAP...but my brain was frozen in the face of way too many options.

What if I searched by customer ratings and quality? Would that make the choice easier? Scanning for plumbers with four and five-star ratings brought the results down to 20. Good progress, I thought, but still too many.

So if searching for proximity didn't solve my problem, and searching for quality didn't solve it either, was there something on their websites that could narrow it down further?

I frantically scanned through the many websites. Could their messaging make one stand out? However, if I expected clarity, I was disappointed.

Page after page said basically the exact same thing. Here are some of the opening headlines I saw:

- We Are Honest, Fast, Reliable
- Trusted Everywhere, Reliable Experts
- Best Trained in The Industry, Your Trust and Satisfaction Is Our #1 Goal
- 20 Years of Experience
- 35 Years of Experience
- Quality Service With Great Rates
- Superior Workmanship at Affordable Prices
- Top Quality Plumbing Services
- Our Mission Is to Provide Excellent and Superior Service!

I quickly noticed a trend: They all touted the exact same message. They each wanted to prove how smart, capable, and qualified they were. And in the moment, I felt overwhelmed, frustrated, and I couldn't tell them apart.

So there I was. In a high-stakes situation, afraid of making a wrong choice, and overwhelmed by too many options. And worse, when I tried to narrow it down by proximity, quality, and messaging, it only became more confusing. I was frantically scrolling, frozen in a state of fear, worry, and indecision.

As I sat there, alone, in the dark, with Lake Surprise oozing through the towels...how do you think I felt?

Drip.

Drip.

Drip.

Suddenly, as if the clouds parted and Angel Gabriel himself had pointed to my computer, I saw a site that said: "24/7 Emergency Service: We Can Fix Any Problem."

Who do you think I immediately called? The "Quality Service With Great Rates" guy? The "35 Years of Experience" guy?

Nope.

As you probably guessed, I dialed the "24/7 Emergency Service" guy, and within 20 minutes a professional was there draining away Lake Surprise. He expertly and cheerfully found the problem, had the tools to solve it, and even pointed out that the damage hadn't been there long enough to ruin the floor. With some airing out and a little repair work, he said, my kitchen would be fine after all. After he left with my heartfelt thanks, I began the tedious process of drying the kitchen and cleaning up the mess. As I mopped and cleaned over the next few hours, I had time to think.

What I realized was this: In hindsight, any one of those plumbers could have solved my *first* problem, which was a flooded kitchen and broken pipes. They were all probably very smart, capable, qualified, and passionate, and their Achievement Mindset messaging proved that point.

However, as I was frantically searching for help, it was clear that a variety of factors simultaneously converged to create an unexpected *second and more urgent* problem: How to choose from an overwhelming amount of high-quality candidates? It was clear that the plumbers were all prepared to address my *first* problem (broken pipes), but most of them were completely unprepared for the *second and more urgent* problem of having to stand out from the crowd.

The game had changed, and they had no idea. Success was no longer about proving they were capable and qualified; it now depended on being chosen over everyone else. And because they had no idea the game had changed, their experience, qualifications, and passion hindered—not helped—their chances of success.

All except the "24/7 Emergency Service" guy. Not only was he prepared for my first problem, but his brand message was positioned and prepared for my *second and more urgent* problem. He knew that people (like me) would reach out for plumbing help in emergencies. He knew that I would be overwhelmed by the vast amount of similar messaging from his competitors. He knew I would be struggling, worried, and afraid. And so his brand messaging was positioned to match my moment.

His message rose above the noise.

His message stood out from the crowd.

And so, he was chosen...over everyone else.

❝His brand messaging was positioned to match my moment. ❞

The Selective Environment

All the other plumbers were living, working, and presenting their message in the Performance Environment. They thought the Achievement Mindset would bring them success, just like it had elsewhere in life. And so their individual branding featured how smart, capable, qualified, and passionate they each were.

However, in those brief moments, I experienced a unique set of factors that completely changed the game. Since everyone else was doing the exact same thing, their messages failed to stand out, and I was overwhelmed, confused, and frustrated. And so their messaging got lost in the noise.

I was no longer in the Performance Environment where success is based on how well you perform. I was in the Selective Environment, where success is based on influencing people to choose you.

THE PERFORMANCE ENVIRONMENT:	THE SELECTIVE ENVIRONMENT:
Where Success Is Based on How Well You Perform	Where Success Is Based on Influencing People to Choose You

So what exactly needs to happen for the Selective Environment to exist? To put it simply, anytime anyone:

1. Has a problem that needs a solution
2. Has to choose an option
3. Has a limited amount of time
4. Is in a situation where the stakes seem high
5. And has an overwhelming number of qualified options to choose from

...they are in the Selective Environment. More specifically, they become "Decision Makers" in the Selective Environment.

However, it's important to understand that Decision Makers aren't just people looking for plumbing help. And the Selective Environment doesn't just occur during Saturday morning emergencies. No, the Selective Environment happens every time your success depends on influencing Decision Makers to choose you over everyone else.

That means college admission reviewers, HR hiring teams, sales leads and prospects, and any other person whose decision determines your success. These are all Decision Makers. And even though they may be from completely different industries and may have completely different roles, when someone faces the five factors listed above, they are in the Selective Environment.

Herein lies our challenge: If your success depends on influencing people to choose you over others, what stands in the way? What are the obstacles that limit your ability to rise above the noise? More importantly, how do Decision Makers make decisions in the Selective Environment?

To start, we need to take a step back and understand how the brain works and what happens when we make decisions—especially in overwhelming situations. Before we can even begin crafting a message that is designed to stand out from the crowd, we need to know the obstacles and hidden pitfalls that lie in our path.

Because in order to reach Decision Makers' hearts and minds, we need to first understand how they think and feel...especially when they are overwhelmed by an abundance of choices.

The World's Greatest Supercomputer

Your brain is the greatest supercomputer ever created. Not only can it learn, adapt, and help you figure out math homework; it does so much more. Every time you stand, walk, or run it silently completes gravity-defying physics and expertly manages sophisticated physical mechanics.

Anytime you breathe, eat, or catch a cold, it flawlessly executes a vast array of complex bodily functions to keep your systems operational.

Not only does your brain manage the hidden functions of your body, but it also processes the information you consume. According to one 2008 study (and how times have changed since then!), if you compile all the "digital information" (i.e. Internet, audio, text, and video) that we consume on a daily basis, the average American consumes over 34 GB of data every single day.[1] To put that into perspective, if you were to watch Netflix at the high-definition stream rate of 5 MBPS, it would take you over 16 hours to stream 34 GB worth of data. And yet you normally consume that much data (and more!) in less than half the time.

By any measurement, that is a staggering amount of work for your brain...in just one day of living! And it does this day in and day out for your entire life.

But this is really only half of the picture.

Science is only beginning to scratch the surface of the capabilities and power of the human brain. But one thing is clear: At the end of the day, that three-pound mass of 86.1 billion[2] neurons has one goal and one goal only: to keep you alive.

Aside from the thankless, subconscious tasks of regulating your heartbeat, triggering your diaphragm to take in air, and a host of other hidden functions, your brain is also working with your conscious mind to constantly monitor the natural environment around you for two things: threats and opportunities.[3] The world can be a dangerous place, and your brain has defenses at the ready. When a dog jumps at you threateningly, when you trip and fall, when you see that snake coiled and ready to strike; your brain adjusts with lightning speed and focuses on the threat.

On the other hand, when you encounter a smiling person, a delicious looking cake, or anything else that helps you live and thrive, your brain is wired to focus on what is important. In other words, according to some researchers, the areas of the brain that determine threats and opportunities "team up with the brain regions that help us pay attention."[3]

And so, as you go about your day, your brain is constantly looking out for threats and opportunities and helping you stay alive by focusing on what is most important. But what if your brain encounters something that is neither a threat nor an opportunity?

It becomes noise.

How The Brain Blocks Noise

Here is where our discussion about Decision Makers and the Selective Environment really gets interesting. The amazing thing is that even though your brain is executing this extraordinary amount of work day in and day out, your conscious mind barely notices any of it. That's because one of the greatest skills your brain has is the ability to filter.

Imagine for a moment you are reading a book outside in a noisy park. Aside from the words on the page, your brain is also taking in every last detail around you. The swaying leaves in the trees, the cars passing by, the birds overhead...But your conscious mind hardly notices any of the distractions because your brain has learned to intentionally filter them out.

In a study published in *Nature Communications*, three scientists found that your brain has an actual "gating mechanism"[4] that controls the flow of thoughts. That's right, in order for something to grab your conscious attention, stimuli must first pass through a series of gates that block or allow certain thoughts.

If a piece of information is important (threat or opportunity), it is allowed to continue to other parts of the brain that lead to decision and action. If it's unimportant (noise), the "gate" shuts and blocks the signal from distracting the brain, thus enabling you to focus on what matters while ignoring everything else.

Dr. Xiao-Jing Wang, Global Professor of Neural Science at NYU and NYU Shanghai put it this way: "It is critical to our everyday life that our brain processes the most important information out of everything presented to us...Without filtering out the most important information, we would be constantly distracted and unable to focus and function. Hence the brain must be able to route relevant information to the right place at the right time."[4]

In other words, your brain is programmed and designed to focus on what is important and ignore the vast majority of insignificant things all around you.

Threat, opportunity, and noise.

Thousands upon thousands of times.

All day, every day.

Bringing It Full Circle

Now, you may be wondering what all this "brain talk" has to do with our discussion about the Selective Environment. Well, it has EVERYTHING to do with it.

Now that we understand that:

- Your brain processes an extraordinary amount of information every day
- It is wired to notice threats and opportunities and ignore everything else
- It has developed formidable filters to block vast amounts of unimportant information

We are left with the most important question at the heart of the Selective Environment:

If your success depends on getting people to choose you, what if Decision Makers encountered not just one or two opportunities, but rather faced an overwhelming number of positive options to choose from? What happens when your enthusiastic and sincere Achievement Mindset message sounds just like everyone else's?

"Your brain is programmed to focus on what is important and ignore the vast majority of insignificant things all around you."

That's when opportunities—something your brain would normally pay attention to in smaller numbers—become noise.

The Brain (And Emotions) in The Selective Environment

This is the fundamental problem that Decision Makers have in the Selective Environment.

That's because whether they are college Admissions reviewers reading piles of essays, HR reps completing endless rounds of interviews, or business prospects sifting through hundreds of marketing brochures, they all have to wade through an overwhelming number of candidates who all sound nearly the same. And try as they might, the more they review, the more difficult it becomes to make decisions.

But why? Why is this all so hard? What exactly is going on inside the brain of a Decision Maker in the Selective Environment?

It turns out that there is A LOT happening, and we can learn a great deal from this.

As we have covered, the brain is accustomed to running a streamlined operation where information is efficiently divided between threat, opportunity, and noise. When it is presented with an abundance of opportunities, this creates the condition that researchers call the "Choice Overload Phenomenon," where "increasing the number of options makes decisions more complex and hence more difficult and frustrating."[5]

To put it simply, when the brain is overloaded with choice, it doesn't quite know what to do.

Over the past several decades, researchers have made some fascinating discoveries that provide critical insights into how people make decisions while experiencing "Choice Overload". And these lessons apply directly to the Selective Environment.

Let's consider three studies and their implications.

Thoughts Are Jammed

In one 2000 study, researchers measured what happened when over 500 shoppers in an upscale grocery store were presented with a tasting booth display featuring an assortment of different flavors of jams.[6] Sometimes the shoppers were presented with a small number of options, and other times the researchers presented a large number of options. In each case, shoppers were invited to taste test the different jams while researchers observed the shoppers' reactions.

It turned out that when shoppers were presented with a small selection of featured jams, they were more likely to purchase one. However, when researchers offered a large selection of jams, people had decreased motivation to make a purchase. "The findings from this study show that an extensive array of options can at first seem highly appealing...yet can reduce [people's] subsequent motivation."[6] The researchers went on to point out that too many options can create uneasiness and fear of making the wrong decision—especially in higher stakes situations.

In other words, when our brain is presented with an abundance of options, it is difficult to process, and our brain wants to avoid it all together. Hence the decreased motivation and feelings of unease and fear.

But there is more.

Too Many Choices, So Little Time

In another study in 2009, nearly 70 college students were presented with the task of selecting a single $100 prize out of several options that were also valued at roughly $100.[5] For example, these included things like gift cards to restaurants, VIP passes to exclusive clubs, and cash cards at popular stores. The difference was that one set of participants was given a small set of options, and another group was presented with a large selection of options to choose from. Simple enough, right? But here is where the researchers made things more difficult.

"When our brain is presented with an abundance of options, it is difficult to process, and our brain wants to avoid it all together."

You see, instead of just testing how people make decisions between small and large selections of choices (as we read about in the first study above), the researchers also wanted to know how *time constraints* impacted the decision-making process. Both the "small set" and "large set" groups were randomly divided further so that some were given two minutes to make a decision (limited time), and others were given five minutes to make their choice (an extended period of time).

What did the researchers find?

First, students who had the challenge of deciding between a large number of options found the task *more difficult* and *frustrating* than those who had a smaller number of options.

However, the second important observation was that having a *limited amount of time* exacerbated the negative emotions even further. Students who had two minutes to decide between abundant options not only found it exponentially more difficult, but their frustration levels increased, and they described the process to be much more complex.

Are we beginning to see a familiar picture? Overwhelming choices and limited time constraints lead to unease, decreased motivation, and frustration.

But it doesn't end there.

Brain Waves...Goodbye

In a third study in 2018, neuroscientists wanted to see what was going on inside of the brain while participants were deciding between different amounts of choices.[7] And so, with electrodes strapped to their heads measuring their brain activity, participants were presented with low, intermediate, and high numbers of choices to choose from. What the scientists discovered is fascinating.

They found that when the brain encountered a high number of items to choose from, something curious happened. Instead of engaging and working through the high variety of choices, the brain did the exact opposite: It significantly decreased activity. Rather than lighting up, the brain activity went dark, indicating the decision-making process was now much more difficult for the participants. In other words, when presented with too many choices, the brain determined the process too costly, became overwhelmed, and "shut down".

Dr. Elena Reutskaja, one of the researchers of the study, summarized her findings: "More choice is better up to a certain point, after which [it] becomes overwhelming and decision-making is impaired."[8]

Your Brain Has Limits

Now that we've delved into some deep research, let's take a step back, come up for air, and drive home why all of this matters for our discussion.

When Decision Makers in the Selective Environment are faced with an overwhelming number of options to choose from, their brains begin to be stressed, overwhelmed, frustrated, and they might even shut down. From all that we have learned, these are not things that the efficient and effective brain likes to feel. What this research suggests is that even though the brain:

- Is immensely capable
- Has evolutionarily designed filters in place to simplify its job
- And is wired to pay attention to key threats and opportunities

...when it is presented with an abundance of comparable choices, something completely different happens. Normally it expertly and nimbly guides you through the extraordinarily complex world we live in. Normally it comfortably executes thousands of commands without breaking a sweat.

But faced with an abundance of options?

Having to make complex decisions in limited amounts of time?

Having to weigh opportunities in high-stakes decisions?

These aren't the simple tasks of figuring out threats, opportunities, and noise that your brain is wired to excel at. These kinds of problems require a great deal of mental work, complex thinking, and analysis to sort out. In other words, your brain goes into *overload* to solve these kinds of problems.

The challenge is this: In the Selective Environment, all these "overload" problems don't just happen one by one. No, they all occur simultaneously and compound into a perfect neural storm the Decision Maker's brain desperately wants to avoid. And, just like my experience in frantically choosing plumbers, the brain feels stressed, frustrated, overwhelmed, unmotivated, and it even sometimes shuts down.

And your message (as well as every other candidate's message) is only making it worse.

Here's What You Are (Really) up Against

When your success is on the line and you are in a "make it or break it" moment, you need to know that when you submit your college application, when you go into that job interview, or when you try to win that client:

- Your message is adding, not detracting, to an increasingly chaotic environment where the Decision Maker feels stressed, overwhelmed, and frustrated.

- You are no longer "inside the Tribe" trying to move up in the Performance Environment. Instead, you are an outsider trying to get in, and proving you are smart, capable, qualified, and passionate does not make you appear as the clear and logical choice. Rather, because everyone else is doing the exact same thing, it undermines your chances and comes across as compounding, confusing noise.

- And finally, you are not just competing against other candidates. You are really competing against millions of years of evolutionary neuro programming that has designed the Decision Maker's brain to disengage, avoid, and ignore your message.

So what are you to do? When your future hinges on your application, interview, or pitch, how can you bypass the brain's defenses and reach the hearts and minds of Decision Makers?

How can you position yourself in a way that shows your message really is an opportunity, and not noise?

How can you stand out when everyone else is trying to stand out too?

You need a new approach.

You need a new language.

You need...the Influence Mindset.

Summary

- In the Selective Environment, Decision Makers have a *second and more urgent problem* of deciding from an abundance of options.
- The brain is immensely powerful. It is designed to pay attention to threats and opportunities and to filter out noise.
- When the brain has an abundance of options to choose from, this is called "Choice Overload".
- When the brain experiences "Choice Overload" it feels stressed, frustrated, overwhelmed, and it can even shut down completely.
- When your brand message is just like everyone else's, it compounds this stressful state for Decision Makers.
- Decision Makers' brains are designed by millions of years of evolutionary neuro programming to disengage, avoid, and ignore your message.

Bonus

For more details and exercises on this chapter head over to: **TheChristianHansen.com/BookBonus**

Situation:	PERFORMANCE ENVIRONMENT	SELECTIVE ENVIRONMENT
Definition:	Success is based on how well you perform	Success is based on influencing people to choose you
Primary Goal:	Prove you are smart, capable, qualified, and passionate	Influence someone to choose you over others
Strategy:	Achievement Mindset	Influence Mindset
?	?	?
?	?	?
?	?	?
?	?	?
?	?	?

SECTION 2:

POSITIONING

The Small Catalog
That Made a Big Difference

"Great things are done by a series of small things
brought together."
—**Vincent Van Gogh**

Richard Warren Sears had a brilliant idea, but he wasn't sure it would work.

It was the late 19th century and farmers in America's heartland were clamoring for the latest comforts available to city folk. Mass production and new inventions were booming in the coastal urban areas, but most people in farm country struggled to get ahold of the latest gadgets.

A few years earlier, a man by the name of Aaron Montgomery Ward had the brilliant idea to start a revolutionary type of business based on a mail-order catalog. Customers would simply choose what they wanted from a printed list of supplies, and he would ship it to them at a significantly reduced price. No physical store meant less overhead expenses, and mailing directly to the customers meant they didn't have to waste time travelling to distant cities.

It was a win-win for everyone.

Business boomed and Montgomery Ward, along with his famous catalog, became a household name across America. Richard Sears, who already had a successful business selling wholesale watches, wanted in on the action.

But how could he enter the already saturated market and stand out? He could easily duplicate the business model, but Sears knew he couldn't win on price or variety of goods. He could also use the same postal service as Ward, but that meant Sears couldn't win on faster delivery times. He and Montgomery Ward were evenly matched in every area. So how was he going to stand out?

The answer? Positioning.

His big idea was this: What if the Sears catalog was slightly smaller than the Montgomery Ward catalog? That's correct, you read that right. His big idea was a small solution.

Now wait a second. How would the catalog size make any difference to his ability to stand out? That's because Richard Sears had a secret weapon: He knew exactly what was going on in the mind of the Decision Makers he wished to influence.

Having grown up on a farm himself, Richard Sears knew that the first rule of any housewife was to have a neat and tidy home. And if there were several catalogs that needed to be organized, the smallest one would naturally go on top. That meant that when millions of housewives across the country organized their homes, the Sears catalog would be *positioned* to be the first one they turned to.

And Sears was right.

It wasn't price or quality that made the difference. It was positioning. He positioned his message to be chosen every time. And gradually, this, and many other smart decisions, meant that over time Sears steadily eclipsed the star of Montgomery Ward.[1]

Today, the same concept applies to college applicants, career seekers, professionals, and entrepreneurs: How you position yourself (and your message) makes all the difference in the Selective Environment.

If you know what is going on in the hearts and minds of your Decision Makers, you can begin to craft your message so it will naturally rise to the top of the pile.

The World's Most Valuable Resource

Have you ever wondered what the world's most valuable resource is? You might immediately think it is something like water, power, gold, or oil. And while those are indeed important, I would argue that companies the world over are spending hundreds of billions of dollars each year to secure one thing and one thing only: your attention.

Remember in the previous chapter when we discussed how your brain is constantly processing increasingly vast amounts of information? All that work hasn't just happened without some drawbacks. Some experts now hypothesize that "Neurologically, our brains are adapting to increasing volumes and velocities of information by shortening attention spans."[2]

That's right, thanks to the hundreds of billions of dollars spent in the global advertising arms race each year, we are all mentally paying for it with an increasing generational attention deficit. And this has consequences in the Selective Environment. Not only are you working against millions of years of neuro programming designed to ignore your message, but you are also competing against a rising tide of digital advertisements and smartphone notifications that are also trying to occupy the Decision Maker's attention. In the midst of this informational battlefield, how can your message get through the chaos and signal to the Decision Maker's brain that you are an opportunity worthy of its attention?

As it turns out, all is not lost.

Despite drowning in a wash of information, your anciently designed brain is still reliably chugging away and looking for threats and opportunities. And, just like Richard Sears, there are several simple things you can do that will optimally position your message and help you capture attention. To do this, we need to know what to expect in the Selective Environment. This leads us to the three key questions.

The Three Key Questions

No matter who you are or what your goals are, Decision Makers will always ask you to answer three essential questions in the Selective Environment:

1. What drives you?
2. What are your credentials?
3. Why this Tribe?

That's it. Without fail, you can take nearly any interview question, college essay prompt, or client's inquiry and fit them into one of these three buckets. And your success hinges on how well you answer them. The problem is that most people don't know how to position and sell themselves. And so their answers to these questions usually sound just like everyone else's, and they get lost in the noise.

Which presents you with two options:

1. You can either take the approach of the Achievement Mindset and spin your wheels trying to prove you are smart, capable, qualified, and passionate (just like everyone else), or
2. You can create a brand message and a game plan (in advance) that is designed to increase your chances of success.

Because let me tell you a secret: The ability to stand out isn't reserved for a select few who are just "born" that way. No, cultivating influence is both an art and a science built on concrete principles that anyone can learn, practice, and improve over time. Over the next few chapters you are about to learn how to intentionally (and subtly) craft a message that is designed to capture attention, establish credibility, and cultivate influence.

And position yourself for success every single time.

CHAPTER 3

Why Pursuing Your Passions Is The Worst Idea!

"The two most important days in your life are the day you are born and the day you find out why."
—Mark Twain

What if I told you there is one simple strategy that anyone can use that is guaranteed to grab attention, hook people to your message, and make you stand out from over 70% of the competition? Better yet, what if I told you that this strategy is based on a single piece of (counterintuitive) advice that goes against everything you've ever been taught about achieving success?

Are you ready? Here it is:

Whatever you do, don't pursue your passions.

You read that correctly.

Don't pursue your passions.

I know this flies in the face of every well-meaning piece of advice you've ever heard, and it makes me sound like the most heartless, insensitive person in the world. But before you shut this book and throw it away, let me explain.

The First Key Question: What Drives You?

When a Decision Maker is determining whether or not to let you into their Tribe, the first question they have is: What drives you? In other words, "What are your motivations?" Normally this takes the form of other questions like, "What excites you?" "What do you enjoy doing?" or even, "Tell me your story." Whatever version the question takes, you can be 100% confident that some form of these questions will always be asked in the Selective Environment.

But here is where most candidates make their first mistake.

From my experience reviewing and interviewing thousands of candidates, I learned that most of the time when answering this question, the first thing out of people's mouths is that they are "passionate" about something.

- "I am really passionate about music."
- "I am passionate and love everything about sport."
- "I have a passion for helping customers."
- "I have a passion for analytics."

And these kinds of statements don't just occur in college essays or job interviews. They are also found in business marketing, sales presentations, and ads just about everywhere.

- "We have a passion for providing the best customer service."
- "Our company has a passion for innovative tech solutions."
- "We are passionate about providing the highest quality of... (insert your choice of words here)."

Passion this, passion that.

Wash, rinse, repeat.

Do these sound familiar at all? More importantly, have you ever used these kinds of statements? I know I have.

These phrases, and others like it, fill countless college essays, interview responses, and marketing pitches in the quest to stand out. However, there are (at least) three problems when your message is driven and shaped by a passion.

Problem #1: "Passion" Is Overused

Remember, the definition of the Achievement Mindset is:

ACHIEVEMENT MINDSET:

Belief That Success Is Based on Proving You Are Smart, Capable, Qualified, and Passionate

As we have covered, the Achievement Mindset works in the Performance Environment. When you are a member of the Tribe, being "passionate" about something usually is all you need to succeed. And so many people mistakenly throw the word passion around as much as possible in the false belief that it will bring them success. But remember, we are not operating in the Performance Environment; we are outside of the Tribe...in the Selective Environment. And as we have learned, if your message is just like everyone else's, you will fail. That's why the Influence Mindset has a different goal in the Selective Environment:

INFLUENCE MINDSET:

Belief That Success Is Based on Influencing People to Select You Over Others

Do you see how this shifts your focus? While the Achievement Mindset is all about proving your capabilities to others, the Influence Mindset is all about capturing attention and influencing others to choose you. If your goal is to first influence Decision Makers to select you over others, then all of a sudden leading with "passion" doesn't quite make sense—because that is what everyone else is doing.

You need a different angle.

❝Leading with "passion" doesn't quite make sense— because that is what everyone else is doing.❞

Problem #2: "Passion" Isn't Specific

How many times have you heard or used the phrase, "I am passionate about helping people." Or maybe, "I am passionate about working with people." I know I have. The problem is, sincere as the sentiment may be, it is a completely *useless* phrase because it is not nearly specific enough to make your message definable and clear. Consider the following:

- A firefighter likes his job because he is passionate about helping people.
- A therapist likes her job because she is passionate about helping people.
- A member of the military may like her job because she is passionate about helping people.

Do you notice a theme? Even though these are three completely different careers, they describe themselves in the exact same way. What these candidates are really trying to say is that they are nice human beings who enjoy helping people. The problem is that Decision Makers are overwhelmed by hundreds of other people who are also perfectly nice human beings. Hence, proving you are a nice person simply compounds the *second and more urgent problem* of having too many options to choose from.

And "wanting to help or work with people" isn't the only example of an overgeneralized "passion" statement. There are many other passion statements that people frequently use to try to stand out. For example:

- "I am passionate about technology." Do you mean computer programming? Aerospace engineering? Website design?
- "I am passionate about the arts." Do you mean art education? Performing music? Sculpture? Mixed media?
- "I am passionate about health." Do you mean modern medicine? Physical fitness? Dietary science? Mental health?

These passion statements (and many others!) far too often speak in undefinable generalities. How can I understand your potential value to my Tribe if your message is way too broad? And when you are trying to stand out against hundreds (if not thousands) of others, a generalized message fails to cultivate the power and influence you need to succeed.

Problem #3: "Passion" Rarely Matches The Moment

When you build your message around describing your passions, it's like offering a hammer to someone who only has a screw. You are essentially offering Decision Makers a solution for a problem they don't have.

Remember my story about Lake Surprise and my frantic search for plumbers? I didn't have a "passion for customer service" problem. I didn't have a "passion for providing superior workmanship" problem. In that moment, I had a "24/7 emergency service" problem. And as a Decision Maker who had a limited amount of time to choose someone in a high-stakes situation, I chose the person whose message matched my moment.

Think about college reviewers, job interviewers, or even the people you are trying to attract as clients. Not only do you need to think about who they are, but you also need to think about the moment they are in when they are making a decision about you. Does proving you are passionate meet them meaningfully in that moment?

- Does proving you are passionate simplify the job of a college reviewer who is up to their ears in thousands of other "passionate" applications?
- Does proving you are passionate clarify the choices for an HR job interviewer who has 20 other phone interviews that day?
- Does proving you are passionate make life easier for a potential client who has been bombarded with calls and emails from your competitors?

The answer to each of these is an obvious no.

When a Decision Maker is trying to figure out who to let into the Tribe, "passions" rarely solve their *second and more urgent problem* of having too many choices to choose from. In the Selective Environment, proving you are passionate only serves to confuse and distract.

Because the game has changed, and passion ultimately fails to match the moment.

Don't pursue your passions. Not only is it one of the worst pieces of advice, but it completely fails you in the Selective Environment.

We need to raise the bar, and help you sharpen your message.

We need a strategy that is guaranteed to make you stand out.

" Proving you are passionate only serves to confuse and distract. "

We need a plan to help you rise above the chaos of choice overload and clearly signal to the Decision Maker's brain that YOU are the one to choose.

Instead of pursuing your passions, I want you to pursue problems you are *passionate about solving*.

The Answer: Problem Focused Passions

What exactly is a Problem Focused Passion? Simply put, it is when you frame your message around a passion for solving a specific problem that affects a specific group of people. Let's take the list of passions we listed earlier to show what I mean:

What Drives You?

ACHIEVEMENT MINDSET	INFLUENCE MINDSET
Passion	*Problem Focused Passion*
"I have a passion for analytics."	"Entrepreneurs can't see the hidden trends in their data, and so they miss opportunities. **I am passionate about analytics** as a way to help future small businesses increase their profitability and impact."
"Our company has a passion for innovative tech solutions."	"Most schools are overwhelmed with the changing landscape of tech, and so they fall behind. **Our company has a passion for innovative tech solutions** as a way to help schools affordably provide the best education."
"I am passionate about working with people."	"People are afraid of hospitals and medical procedures, and it impairs their ability to get critical help. **I am passionate about working with people** to help them feel comfortable and confident while receiving health care."

Can you see how the overgeneralized passion statements on the left are weak when compared to the ones framed by a problem on the right? In each case, the passion is transformed to solve a specific problem for a specific group of people. This is the first step to building a message that is designed to capture attention and cultivate influence.

Some Real-world Examples

Below are some examples of normal "passions" compared to times where people harnessed the power of Problem Focused Passions.

Student Example: Achievement Mindset

I once read a college admissions essay that was all about proving the student was passionate:

"I am passionate about music. I have been studying the violin for over 10 years, and feel as if time flies when I am performing. The joy and wonder found in music is absolutely amazing! I love the feeling when I've touched the heart of another, and know that music brings joy to all who listen. This truly is my passion, and I know that's what I want to do in my life: perform music for others."

From my perspective, there was nothing wrong with that essay; it was perfectly fine. But the thing is, I also had hundreds of other perfectly fine essays from perfectly fine students. They were all using Achievement Mindset language to say similar things, and so this student didn't really stand out.

Student Example: Influence Mindset

Now compare the first essay with an essay from a completely different student:

"Social media consumes a lot of my friends, and I can't help but notice how many high schoolers my age are depressed because we are constantly comparing ourselves to each other. I think many of us have really unhealthy emotional lives. Music, however, has been an outlet where I have been able to escape the oppressive demands of social media. There I feel more confidence, I can work towards my goals, and I feel happier. I think music has a special way of helping us connect with our emotions in a healthy way, and I am passionate about using music to help future teenagers build healthy emotional habits. I want to be a music educator to use music as a way to help the next generation of students build positive mental and emotional health in the midst of such a toxic social media fueled culture."

If you were a Decision Maker and had to choose one, who would you choose? Student #1 who is really passionate about music? Or Student #2 who wants to use music as a way to solve the pervasive emotional health crisis caused by social media? Though Student #1 was an excellent student and spent her time proving how capable and qualified she was, Student #2 stood out because instead of only a passion, she had a Problem Focused Passion. And that made her message more influential than the first.

Career Example: Achievement Mindset

I once interviewed a group of candidates applying for an internship in a large company. They all had similar credentials and had graduated from competitive universities. However, when I asked the question, "Talk to me about your professional interests," the overwhelming majority of them spoke of their passions. Some spoke about their passion for efficiency. Others focused on their passion for making things that have the finest quality, and some talked about how they were passionate about doing the best work possible. "I am passionate about making the finest appliances in the world at this company!" one eagerly shared.

Like Student #1 in the first example, those responses are perfectly fine. But they all sounded the same. Again, they were trying to prove that they were smart, capable, and qualified. But none of their messaging was able to solve the *second and more urgent problem*: how to stand out from each other.

Career Example: Influence Mindset

Compare their Achievement Mindset answers to the response I received from another candidate:

"I grew up in a poor town where many families couldn't afford the appliances that this company produces. However, when I left for university, I moved to a larger city where most people could afford these amazing appliances that made life much easier. Right now, many of the products here are still too expensive for many people in my hometown, but the more efficient we make them, the more affordable they can one day become. So, I am passionate about efficiency like everyone else here, but I am passionate about efficiency because I see it as a way to help poor families live easier lives. And not just those in my hometown, but in other countries as well."

If you had to choose one, who would you choose? Most would select the second, and I agree. Again, it's not that he has more impressive credentials, but rather that his message simply stands out from the crowd. One reason being that his message is driven by a Problem Focused Passion.

Professional Example: Achievement Mindset

When I went through the process of buying a home for the first time, I had to decide between several loan officers my real estate agent recommended. As I "interviewed" each one, most of them gave classic "Achievement Mindset" answers, and I struggled to really see much of a difference between them. "I am passionate about getting people the best loan rates possible," one said. Another mentioned, "I think I'm a great choice because I'm the numbers nerd on my team and really love market analysis. Plus, making sure that my clients feel they are getting the best deals out there is what I like most."

The others I met with pretty much said similar things. Even though they were all capable and qualified, to my brain experiencing "Choice Overload", they all seemed to be the same.

Professional Example: Influence Mindset

But imagine how different it was when I met someone who framed it this way: "Look," they said, "buying a home is stressful enough, and most of the time lining up the financing is an additional hassle that most people don't think about until it's too late. I love helping people get into their dream home, and it's my goal to make the difficult process as simple and easy as possible. Of course, you will get the best rates available, but more importantly, I'm going to be there every step of the way to make sure the process is as painless as possible."

Again, this person framed their message around a Problem Focused Passion and they clearly stood out compared to all the others who only used the Achievement Mindset. And so, they won my business.

Problem Focused Passion = Purpose

In each of these examples, the bigger question we should ask is: Why? How come when we take a regular "passion" and upgrade it to a "Problem Focused Passion" we are we more drawn to it? What about Problem Focused Passions makes them more influential and powerful than mere passions?

To put it simply, when you have a Problem Focused Passion, you have a purpose. And having a purpose is the first step towards truly standing out.

One Stanford-based researcher discovered that only 20% of young adults from the age of 12 to 22 have a sense of what their purpose in life is and why.[1] And the statistics aren't much better for when college graduates reach the workforce. According to another study, only 28% of professionals in the US are purpose oriented, and the remaining 72% have their careers solely for financial gain and extrinsic rewards.[2]

This means that when you position yourself as a person with a purpose (that aligns with the Tribe), you automatically stand apart from 80% of students and over 70% of the workforce. And when the majority of candidates in the Selective Environment have no clue what they are doing and why, having a purpose will give you a competitive edge.

But the benefits don't end there.

That's because when you frame your purpose around solving a specific problem, some magical things begin to happen inside the brain. Specifically, there are at least four major reactions that occur in the hearts and minds of Decision Makers that can be used to your advantage.

Because, as we will soon discover, the brain is wired to be influenced by purpose.

Let's take a look at what these four advantages are and how they increase your chances of success in the Selective Environment.

Advantage #1: Purpose, Novelty, and The Brain

In the Selective Environment, most people use overgeneralized passion statements to answer "What drives you?" And if everyone else is floundering with directionless messages, framing your passion around solving a specific problem is a novel approach.

There are several advantages here.

First, your brain is wired to pay attention to novelty.[3] When your message is uniquely framed around solving a problem, Decision Makers are less likely to dismiss, ignore, and move past your message. And in the Selective Environment, more attention is guaranteed to increase your chances.

That's because when the brain encounters something new and interesting, it releases dopamine, which is the "feel good" chemical.[4] And your brain LOVES dopamine. Think about when you have some chocolate. Or that extra piece of cake. Or maybe you can remember the thrill you felt on a roller coaster ride. All of those feelings are caused by, you guessed it, dopamine.

And our brain can't get enough of it.

" When the majority of candidates have no clue what they are doing and why, having a purpose will give you a competitive edge. "

That's why we enjoy what researchers call "novelty seeking".[3] Have you ever been travelling and wanted to explore a delightful-looking road you didn't notice before? Have you been on a hike and wanted to take a path to just see what was over the next hill? Maybe you heard an interesting story and wanted to hear more. Your brain is hooked on discovering new things, and just like that cake, chocolate, and rollercoaster, when our brain encounters something new and interesting, it releases dopamine.

In other words, our brains are wired to seek and pay attention to new and novel things, and if the Selective Environment is flooded with a sea of people boasting about their overgeneralized passions? Then when Decision Makers encounter your novel problem-focused message, their brains are wired (and even addicted) to be intrigued.[3]

So while everyone else's Achievement Mindset message is creating noise and being ignored, you can make your candidacy an attention-grabbing, dopamine-rewarding experience. Pretty cool, right?

Advantage #2: Purpose and Positivity Is Contagious

The next benefit that comes from having a Problem Focused Passion is emotional contagion. Do you know someone whose personality "lights up a room?" Or how about a friend whose positive outlook always cheers you up? Their influence is partly caused by emotional contagion, which is when emotions can spread and be contagious to others.[5]

Here's where having a Problem Focused Passion comes into play. If you are passionate about solving something, it generally means you have a positive view that the problem can be solved. It means you've taken a good hard look at what the problem is and are confident that there is a solution. You are saying, "We can do this!" And your optimism and positivity shine through your message and influence others too.

But emotion isn't the only thing that is contagious...purpose is contagious too. As we will cover in a later chapter, when we encounter someone who has and is actively pursuing a purpose, we are also likely to buy into their message and relate to them.

"Your brain is wired to pay attention to novelty."

So while the Decision Maker's brain could be experiencing the frustrating, debilitating, and overwhelming effects of choice overload, the positive and unique approach resulting from your purpose could light up their day. And a happy Decision Maker is a generous Decision Maker.

Better yet, your chances of success just went up.

Advantage #3: Having A Purpose Positions You As A Potential Leader

The third advantage that comes from framing your personal brand around a Problem Focused Passion is that it positions you (and influences people to see you) as a potential leader.

Why is positioning yourself as a leader important?

Decision Makers aren't just looking for the best people for their Tribe, but they are always looking for the best people for the *future* of the Tribe.

As an undergraduate admissions reviewer, I would always ask: How will this person make a difference here on campus? As a graduate admissions rep I would always have in the back of my mind: Does this candidate seem like the type of person who will be engaged as an alumni one day? And in working in the corporate space, upper-level leaders would always ask us to identify candidates who seemed to have leadership potential. At every stage of selection, we value and prefer potential leaders.

Hence, Decision Makers are always looking out for people who have the potential to lead and shape the future of their Tribe. And when you signal that you have a Problem Focused Passion, you demonstrate that you think and view the world differently than 70% of the candidates. That's because one of the traits of leadership is not the ability to solve problems, but rather the ability to identify problems that no one else can see. And so when you use a Problem Focused Passion, you are signaling that you are more desirable and have more potential to impact the future of the Tribe.

But the remarkable correlations between a Problem Focused Passion and leadership don't end there. Studies show that being purpose focused doesn't just influence others to see your leadership potential, but it also means you are statistically more likely to become a leader too. One study found that: "Purpose-Oriented Workers were 55% more likely to hold director positions, 39% more likely to hold vice president or C-level positions, and 50% more likely to be in the top position in their organization."[6] Not only are purpose-oriented people more likely to become leaders, but they are also more likely to grow professionally and offer greater contributions to their organizations over time.

That is why signaling to Decision Makers that you will grow, impact, and lead their organization for years to come will make you stand out.

Can you see how this small shift in messaging from an overgeneralized passion to a Problem Focused Passion changes the whole game? But the benefits continue. As it turns out, the brain is also wired to be influenced by language built on Problem Focused Passions.

"Leadership is not the ability to solve problems, but rather the ability to identify problems that no one else can see."

Advantage #4: Inspirational Communication and Your Brain

When you share a message based on a Problem Focused Passion, you are inviting the Decision Maker to reimagine the future. And when you do this, some amazing things happen inside the brain.

I once interviewed a candidate for an MBA program who spoke about his experience teaching English in foreign countries. "The problem is," he said, "these kids in remote areas are smart, but they simply don't have access to the information. I really think technology can help solve that problem."

He went on to frame his purpose around using an MBA to build partnerships with education tech organizations to increase access to education one day. "Just imagine," he said, "what would it be like for all these kids in these remote parts of the world to have information at their fingertips? It could shape the future of their countries."

Can you visualize those kids learning with computers or tablets? Do you have that image in your mind?

He may not have realized it, but this candidate harnessed one of the most powerful experiences our brain can have: envisioning the future. Which is precisely the power that "charismatic leadership" can have. That's because when we invite people to imagine "how things could be one day," we are actually creating a shared visionary experience where the communicator and listener are transported to see and feel similar emotions.

When the brain pauses to imagine "what things could be like," it lights up in a flurry of activity that activates areas of the brain directly tied to emotions.[7] That means when your message describes solving a problem in the future, people don't only become more altruistic and hopeful, but they are temporarily transported into seeing an actual shared vision you created. In some ways, when you describe a future problem to be solved as part of your purpose, you are able to help the Decision Maker experience and imagine (in real time) what it would be like to solve that problem.

What an amazing possibility!

So not only does framing your purpose around solving a future problem signal to Decision Makers that you have charismatic leadership potential, but it also triggers this immensely powerful mechanism that makes people more disposed to like and trust you.

But the implications don't end there.

When you speak the language of charismatic leadership and convey images of solving a future problem, you begin to harness the power of inspirational communication. One study found that when participants listened to inspirational messages from people they perceived as leaders, their brains went into a state of "increased activation"[8] and they were more likely to be influenced.

Furthermore, being perceived as charismatic can actually disarm the formidable defenses of skeptical Decision Makers. Another study found that when participants interacted with someone they perceived to be charismatic, their neuro defenses (which normally resist attempts to be influenced by others) were temporarily lowered, making them more susceptible to influence.[9]

Again, can you see how upgrading your passion statement to a Problem Focused Passion completely changes the game in your favor? Just this one subtle shift will help you tap into the powers of charisma and inspirational communication, and this will ultimately help your message rise above the noise.

Let's Recap

It's pretty clear that, despite all the good intentions that come from pursuing your passions, it is ineffective in the Selective Environment. However, when you upgrade your passion into a Problem Focused Passion, everything completely changes.

Just imagine: While your message (which is propelled by your Problem Focused Passion) is:

- Setting you apart from 70 to 80% of the competition
- Capturing attention of Decision Makers with your novel approach
- Releasing dopamine to hook people on your message
- Easing anxiety and frustration through positive emotional contagion
- Signaling your leadership potential and future value to the Tribe
- Transporting Decision Makers to experience your vision of the future
- And lowering neuro defenses to make people like and trust you more

...your competitor's non-specific and overgeneralized passion-driven message merely got stopped, blocked, and ignored.

Just like everyone else's.

Don't pursue your passions.

Rather increase your opportunities and chances for success by harnessing the power of Problem Focused Passions. This will make you stand out in the Selective Environment and add a greater level of power, purpose, resilience, and influence in every other aspect of your life.

Summary

- The first question Decision Makers ask in the Selective Environment is, "What Drives You?"
- Most candidates respond with their passions. The problem is that this answer is overused, not specific, and fails to make you stand out.
- Instead, frame your motivation and purpose around a Problem Focused Passion.
- This shows you have a purpose, and when you have a purpose, the brain is wired to pay attention to you.
- That's because Problem Focused Passions are novel, contagious, shows you as a leader, and makes you seem more inspirational. These effects all release dopamine and influence the brain to like and trust you more.

Bonus

For more details and exercises on this chapter, head over to: **TheChristianHansen.com/BookBonus**

Situation:	PERFORMANCE ENVIRONMENT	SELECTIVE ENVIRONMENT
Definition:	Success is based on how well you perform	Success is based on influencing people to choose you
Primary Goal:	Prove you are smart, capable, qualified, and passionate	Influence someone to choose you over others
Strategy:	Achievement Mindset	Influence Mindset
What Drives You?	Passion	Problem Focused Passion
?	?	?
?	?	?
?	?	?
?	?	?

CHAPTER 4

How to Avoid Being Average

"Logic makes you think. Emotion makes you act."
—**Alan Weiss**

"There has to have been some mistake. Can't you see all the things he has done?"

A few days earlier, our university had released the admissions decisions for the upcoming fall class, and as was customary, my calendar was suddenly filled with urgent appointments from aggrieved parents and students who were upset that they had been denied. In this case, sitting across from me was an agitated father in a well-tailored suit who was insisting something had gone horribly wrong when we didn't admit his son.

"Look," he pressed, leaning forward, "this kid is one of the top athletes in his school. He played varsity football and varsity basketball for the last two years. He is also one of the most service-minded kids in his grade. He participates in clubs and earned an Eagle Scout award for community service. On top of that, he has competitive grades, he's taken AP courses, and he scored above average on his SAT."

The father rattled off several more prestigious accomplishments as if each were to prove the tipping point for my cold heartless soul. As he spoke, I pulled up the student's profile on our system, and indeed, all of these accomplishments had been listed and reviewed by our team. His application essays were recitations of impressive achievements, and he spent a great deal of time describing the awards he had received for various activities. This student clearly had good grades, strong recommendations, and a solid list of accomplishments.

The sad fact was this: I had read hundreds of applications that were nearly identical.

- Varsity sports
- Involvement in the arts
- Service clubs
- High grades
- Faith and community involvement
- Above-average standardized test scores.

All these students had presented their message from the Performance Environment. However, even though each and every one of these students were capable, they were *indistinguishable* because everyone else was using Achievement Mindset strategies too. Hence many smart, capable, qualified, and passionate students were denied.

Then the father said something that really caught my ear: "He is the most well-rounded, capable, and qualified kid I know, and yet somehow you guys don't think he can hack it."

"Sir," I responded, "I have no doubt your son can 'hack it'. He clearly has some impressive achievements, and I'm sure he would succeed here."

Exasperated, he shot back, "Then why did you guys deny him?"

"To be frank," I said, leaning forward as well, "everyone else can hack it too."

He sat back weighing my words.

I continued, "It's clear your son has what it takes. He is obviously an eminently bright and capable individual. But the problem is, we get thousands of applicants who are similarly capable and qualified. We get thousands of applicants who have two varsity sports, competitive grades, and extensive service experiences. We get thousands of students who did well on the SAT and have above average grades..."

"Everyone else can hack it too."

"But in his school," he interjected, "he really is one of the top performers. Doesn't that make him stand out?"

"I'm sure that in his high school he was an outstanding student," I responded, "but in our pool of applicants, being capable and qualified is quite average."

After it was clear his son didn't have grounds for reconsideration, the conversation eased and turned to reapplication strategies for the future. We discussed various options and I helped him create a game plan for his son. As he gathered his things and prepared to leave, he turned and said, "You know, I thought that if we just showed he was a good, capable, and qualified kid, his application would be strong enough. I didn't realize that being outstanding where we are from is only average here."

This well-intentioned father—like countless well-meaning parents across the world—was stuck in the Performance Environment and thought the Achievement Mindset would make his son stand out. He, like many others, assumed that proving his son was smart, capable, qualified, and passionate would bring the success they both hoped for. The problem was that he had no idea that in the Selective Environment, everyone else was trying to do the same thing too.

The game had changed, and his strategy now became a liability.

The Second Key Question: What Are Your Credentials?

In the Selective Environment, after a Decision Maker has asked "What Drives You?", the second major thing they want to know is, "What Are Your Credentials?" Whether in interviews, formal university applications, or introductory conversations to explore business opportunities, Decision Makers essentially want to know what you have done, what you can do, and why they should pay attention to you.

In the Performance Environment, the Achievement Mindset's response to this question usually includes a combination of previous experience, performance indicators, prestige, and percentages. For example, in efforts to prove that they can outperform everyone else, someone might cite a prestigious institution as their educational background. Another might use the weight of their previous experience to bolster their authority. Alternatively, someone might rely on previously achieved performance indicators to prove their point.

What Are Your Credentials?
THE ACHIEVEMENT MINDSET
Previous Experience
Performance Indicators
Prestige
Percentages

At the end of the day, in the Performance Environment, we have learned to see success as the result of an objective, clear-cut, logical decision. Whomever performs best, wins most. And so the person who proves they have the highest accumulation of previous experience, performance indicators, prestige, and percentages naturally wins. Hence, when Decision Makers across the spectrum want to know, "What are your credentials?", we have learned through years and years of training to cram college applications, job interviews, and sales pitches with Achievement Mindset language.

But as we've learned, when a Decision Maker is presented with an abundance of options to choose from, they now have a *second and more urgent problem* of deciding who to choose. We are no longer in the Performance Environment; we are in the Selective Environment. And as the father of the denied college student in the story above discovered, proving you are smart, capable, qualified, and passionate makes you just like everyone else.

In other words, when your message is packed with previous experience, performance indicators, prestige, and percentages in the Selective Environment...it turns to noise.

Performance, Experience, Prestige, and Percentages = Noise

Do you recall the story about Lake Surprise in Chapter 2? There, the plumbers' messages were all based on classic Achievement Mindset answers of previous experience, performance indicators, prestige, and percentages.

And do you remember the result?

As I grappled with the *second and more urgent problem* of deciding who to choose, the plumbers' messaging compounded, not clarified, the problem. And so my brain became completely overwhelmed, frustrated, and stressed, labelling their messages as noise.

As I have mentioned before, this mistake doesn't just affect plumbers (or other entrepreneurs) trying to win new business and stand out from the crowd. This also impacts prospective undergraduate and graduate students, as well as career seekers. Consider the following:

- College applications bulge at the seams with lists of achievements and impressive facts and figures.
- Graduate school applications and interviews are frequently filled with prestigious educational backgrounds as well as arsenals of impressive facts and figures to strengthen their candidacy.
- Job resumes, interviews, and networking events are replete with people persistently sharing percentages and their previous performance achievements.

Across the board, because people mistakenly believe their #1 goal is to prove they can outperform everyone else, they heavily rely on the Achievement Mindset. However, they don't realize that the game has changed and that in the Selective Environment, their Achievement Mindset messaging is impeding, not influencing, the hearts and minds of Decision Makers.

How does the Influence Mindset answer the question, "What are your credentials?" How is its approach different?

It starts by harnessing People Centered Problems.

People Centered Problems

Sitting in the hotel lobby amid the constant flow of people coming in and out of the building, I looked at my watch.

I was in New Delhi representing our program as part of an MBA fair that was set to travel throughout India for the next few weeks. The next day we were to fly south to the leafy canopy-lined streets of Bangalore to meet new groups of students, and then to iconic Hyderabad a few days after that. As graduate school recruiters, one of our goals was to meet top candidates, and I was wrapping up a busy day interviewing prospects from a variety of backgrounds. I had a few minutes before the next person was supposed to show up, and I decided to review my notes from the previous interviews.

The day had been pretty typical.

The candidates had each sat eagerly upright in their starched shirts and pressed suits, crisp copies of their resumes in hand. They proceeded to enthusiastically bury me with an overwhelming number of facts, figures, and achievements from their careers. Most had impressive backgrounds in tech, management consulting, accounting, and other areas. They all had top marks from their undergraduate institutions, and some even had already completed specialized master's degrees. They all were delightful to speak with, polite, polished, and thoroughly professional. I had no doubt that each and every one of these candidates were immensely talented, capable, and would raise the game of any MBA student team they were placed on in our program.

And that was the agonizing problem I faced.

The quality they presented and the brilliance they would bring to our program was unquestionable. However, how could I honestly sift through each and every one of their varied and accomplished resumes and choose one over all the others? They each were so good, so bright, and so capable that I struggled to really know who to recommend to our committee.

In the steady flow of people, I noticed a student cautiously approaching me. As I rose, he extended his hand and introduced himself as my next appointment. As we sat down opposite each other, I noticed his immaculate suit, crisp shirt, and seamless tie...just like everyone else. He politely asked how my day was going and proceeded to hand me his neatly typed resume....just like everyone else.

This was probably going to go just like all the other interviews, I thought.

However, as we began our informal introductory conversation, I noticed that even though his English was occasionally halting, his ideas and ways of phrasing were distinct from the other applicants I had met earlier. As we began, I scanned over his resume and gave the same open-ended invitation I asked all the others: "So, tell me your story."

"In some ways," he began, "I'm probably like your typical MBA candidate. As you can tell from my resume, I did well at my university. I graduated in computer science, and since then I've been working in software development for the past few years—with a few promotions in my department."

I smiled and nodded. "Yup. That is pretty typical."

"But the difference is, instead of recounting the things you can clearly read on my resume, I want to tell you the back story about why I pursued those roles and what my motivations were."

Intrigued by his novel approach, I invited him to continue.

"I love technology, and everything it has brought us," he began, "and at first when I started my education in computer science, I did it because I wanted to learn all there was about computers. But the problem is, tech has advanced almost too quickly and become too complicated. It's like the bat is swinging the cricketer instead of the other way around. Later in my career I noticed that many people in our target audience were not using our software applications as we originally had hoped because, as it turns out, you almost needed a degree in computer science to understand what to do! That was the opposite of what we wanted to accomplish."

"Interesting," I said, "How did you solve this?"

Grateful for the lead-in, he continued, "When I became the team lead, we made it our goal to develop software in a way that made things easier—and not more difficult—for the end user. Instead of starting with the problem (as we saw it), we needed to start with the people and their perspective in mind. And as time progressed, we found this people-centered approach made all the difference."

He then proceeded to walk me through his career from the perspective of how each step started with a People Centered Problem they noticed, and then resulted in concrete benefits for people. "The feedback we received from users was much more positive. Instead of being confused and frustrated, more and more people enjoyed and appreciated the benefits we were trying to provide in the first place."

Hearing this candidate walk through his resume was extraordinary. For the previous several hours, my brain had been subjected to an eye-watering barrage of previous experiences, performance indicators, prestige, and percentages. But this applicant completely changed the game by centering all of his achievements in the context of solving People Centered Problems.

As the conversation continued, I realized something: In all the other interviews, after about five minutes, I had a pretty clear picture of who each person was and was subconsciously looking at my watch, ready for the next interview. But with this candidate, I was intrigued. Each section in his resume revealed a continuously unfolding narrative that I was interested in learning more about.

As the conversation ended, I thanked him for meeting with me, gave him my card, and invited him to reach out once I had returned back to the States. He gratefully accepted and cheerfully headed out into the bustling, noisy city. As I gathered my things and headed to my room to pack for the next day's flight, I mentally reviewed all the students I had met that day. Even though this last candidate was similar to everyone else on paper, it was clear who I would recommend to the committee. He seemed to have much more leadership potential, and I was confident of the impact he would make in our program.

However, I had one looming question. If his qualifications, work experience, and educational achievements were so similar to the others, why did he stand out so much compared to them? Why did he seem to have so much more potential and influence than every other candidate? Though there were many things he did well in his interview, one subtle factor in his approach has become increasingly clear the more I've thought about it. And in the years that have followed, I've seen other master communicators use the exact same tool time and time again.

The answer? Instead of performance indicators, prestige, and percentages, this candidate used People Based Results to solve People Centered Problems.

People Based Results

The brain is wired to ignore noise. And when the brain encounters large amounts of numbers and facts that ultimately are neither opportunities nor threats, the information is labelled as noise and is ignored.

Which is exactly what happened to my brain in most of the interviews that day.

Sure, one or two students who shared impressive lists of performance indicators, prestige, and percentages would have kept my attention and interest. But a whole day filled with the exact same thing? Millions of years of evolutionary neuro programming kicked in (as well as a little boredom induced from all the informational "noise"), and my brain quickly became immune to the attention-seeking potential of each student's impressive array of achievements.

Despite my best efforts, my brain was programmed to label their messages as noise, and I subconsciously started looking at my watch after five minutes.

So why did that last candidate capture my attention so effectively?

Because he framed his credentials around how his previous experiences impacted people. In other words, he used what I call People Based Results. Even though he initially went into computer science because he loved technology, he later noticed that normal people struggled to use his web-based applications because the software was too complicated. His purpose then shifted to focusing on how he could solve this People Centered Problem, and he framed his career narrative around this different perspective. While all the other candidates were trying to persuade me with percentages and performance indicators, he used people. And in the end, his approach was far more effective at capturing my attention and cultivating influence.

What Are Your Credentials?

ACHIEVEMENT MINDSET	INFLUENCE MINDSET
Previous Experience	People Centered Problems
Performance Indicators	↓
Prestige	People Based Results
Percentages	

Why? Why is talking about people more effective?

Because we are wired for stories and connection.

We Are Wired to Pay Attention to What Happens to People

Our brains are simply wired to pay attention to what happens to other people. Some researchers hypothesize that this is the result of hundreds of thousands of years of living in social groups and depending on others for survival.[1] Whatever the reasons, our brains are programmed to pay more attention to people as opposed to things.

Have you ever sat through a presentation that was filled with slide after slide of long chunks of text, graphs, statistics, and numbers? I know I have. And if your experience was even remotely similar to mine, all that dense information passed through your eyes and ears without leaving a trace.

But have you also ever sat through a presentation where a person shared a story about themselves or someone else? Chances are that you paid much more attention and can recall several of the stories off the top of your head. This is because we are wired to pay attention to stories, and we are especially wired to pay attention to stories about people.[2]

❝We are wired for stories and connection.❞

Which is exactly what happened to my brain in that New Delhi hotel lobby.

Though all the other candidates' interviews were filled with performance indicators, prestige, and percentages, they were ultimately about "things" and failed to capture my attention. In fact, thanks to millions of years of programming, my brain was working on overdrive to resist their efforts of distracting and overwhelming me with the abundance of facts. However, the moment the last candidate wrapped his message around People Based Results, he basically created a "Trojan Horse" that bypassed my embattled neural defenses and deployed his message behind the walls with maximum effect.

How was this possible? Why do stories about people influence us more?

This is because of an amazing hormone called oxytocin. Let's take a brief dive into research that will completely change how we look at stories, human connection, and influence.

Oxytocin: The Connection Hormone

A lot of research has come out on the hidden power of oxytocin and its vast influence on our behavior.[3,4] In short, oxytocin is the hormone that fosters social bonding and connection. Have you ever felt gradually close to a new group of people you just met? Or how about those warm fuzzies you felt when you held a newborn baby? Maybe you've felt a special bond with a loved one in your life.

All of these experiences were influenced by the hormone oxytocin. If our brain has been designed to survive by living, working, and connecting in social groups, it needs a mechanism to influence our behaviors towards building and maintaining those social connections. Oxytocin is the tool our brain uses to foster and fortify these important relationships, which explains why we are so effective at creating and maintaining Tribes. While love, newborn babies, and forming social groups are heady examples of what oxytocin is capable of, for our discussion we need to talk about how it gets released, and the amazing chain of events that occurs when oxytocin ricochets through the brain. More importantly, we are going to learn the surprising effects it can have on Decision Makers in the Selective Environment.

It all starts where emotions begin in the brain: the Limbic System.

The Room Where It Happens

The limbic system is located at the center of your brain. Research has found that the limbic system is a collection of neural structures that are primarily responsible for influencing emotion, memory creation, and more.[5] Can you remember a time when you felt safe in the arms of a loved one? Or what about that time when you were really happy after winning a reward? You have your limbic system to thank for those emotion-drenched memories, because while you were feeling those intense feelings and soaking in all the information from your environment, your limbic system was weaving it all together and creating potent memories that you can relive again and again.

Deep inside the limbic system is a tiny organ that packs a big punch: the amygdala. Technically derived from the Latin term for "almond", the amygdala is about the size and shape of...you guessed it...an almond. And you have two of them; one in each hemisphere of your brain. These are important because research has shown that your two amygdalae are the epicenters for your emotions.[6] But they also have some other surprising responsibilities:

- They influence your motivation
- They process emotional learning
- They shape social behavior
- They impact the emotional influences on attention and perception
- They also impact your ability to create social judgements of other people.[7]

Wait a minute.

So, there is a specific part of our brain that influences how we react, pay attention to, perceive, remember, and create judgements of other people? Yes. The amygdala and the limbic system directly influence all of these actions. They are responsible for shaping our connections and opinions of others, and in the Selective Environment, this is exactly what you need for success.

Which raises the question: Is there a way to bypass the brain's defenses and speak directly to the limbic system? If so, what if you could craft a message that was designed to influence Decision Makers to view you more positively?

As it turns out, you can.

In fact, the limbic system (and a Decision Maker's perception of you!) is wired to be strongly influenced by a particularly powerful hormone that is released when we engage with stories about other people. You guessed it: oxytocin.

This Is Your Limbic System on Oxytocin

When we hear stories about people, a remarkable chain reaction begins when oxytocin is released in the amygdala and the limbic system. Not only are people more likely to feel connected with you and lower their mental defenses, but research has also shown that oxytocin can influence people to experience the following things:

- It makes people more generous[8]
- It causes them to act and respond more favorably and responsibly towards others[9,10]
- It reduces anxiety[11]
- It increases empathy[12]
- It transports them out of their current reality into envisioning and experiencing the narrative you create[9]
- It influences them to judge unfamiliar people more positively.[13]

As you let these sink in, let's recap.

When you use the Influence Mindset and wrap your credentials in People Centered Problems that are solved by People Based Results, you are bypassing formidable neuro defenses and triggering the Decision Maker's brain to release oxytocin. This, in turn, influences their limbic system to be more motivated, give your message more attention, feel more empathy, reduce anxiety, become more generous, and improve how they think and feel about you.

And while your message ignites their minds and is creating a neural firework show that captures attention and influences people to choose you, your competitors' messages (filled with percentages, performance indicators, and prestige) are being labelled as noise and ignored.

Can you see how much more impactful the Influence Mindset makes your message? While everyone else is breathlessly trying to prove that they can outperform everyone else, you can subtly shift your message in a way that is more likely to win hearts and minds.

"When we hear stories about people, a remarkable chain reaction begins."

Everyone Else Can Hack It Too

When that distraught and frustrated father said, "...and yet somehow you guys don't think he can hack it," he was clearly thinking and operating in the Performance Environment. He thought proving his son could hack it would bring the success he and his son hoped for. But what he didn't realize was that he was not operating in the Performance Environment. He was really in the Selective Environment, and everyone else he was competing against could hack it too.

The game had changed, and his strategy became a liability.

Which is what the Influence Mindset anticipates. Instead of worrying about proving they are good enough, people operating from the Influence Mindset know that proving percentages, performance indicators, and prestige only compounds the *second and more urgent problem* of having too many choices to choose from. And so, in an effort to stand out from the crowd, the Influence Mindset crafts a message that signals they have desirable qualities that will impact the Tribe.

Which brings us to the third key principle of the Influence Mindset that we will cover in the next chapter. We are about to learn that, while everyone else is trying to focus on survival of the fittest, success really comes when you prove you are the *best fit*.

Welcome to the third key question of the Selective Environment: "Why This Tribe?"

Summary

- The second key question Decision Makers always ask is, "What are your credentials?"
- Most people will respond with previous experience, performance indicators, prestige, and percentages. However, these universal answers don't make you stand out.
- Instead, within the Influence Mindset, people frame their credentials around People Centered Problems and People Based Results.
- This captures attention because we are wired to pay attention to stories about people, and when our brain hears stories about people, it releases oxytocin.
- Oxytocin, in turn, unleashes a host of neural reactions that improves how people perceive you.

Bonus

For more details and exercises on this chapter head over to: **TheChristianHansen.com/BookBonus**

Situation:	PERFORMANCE ENVIRONMENT	SELECTIVE ENVIRONMENT
Definition:	Success is based on how well you perform	Success is based on influencing people to choose you
Primary Goal:	Prove you are smart, capable, qualified, and passionate	Influence someone to choose you over others
Strategy:	Achievement Mindset	Influence Mindset
What Drives You?	Passion	Problem Focused Passion
What Are Your Credentials?	Previous experience, performance indicators, prestige, and percentages	People Centered Problems ↓ People Based Results
?	?	?
?	?	?
?	?	?

CHAPTER 5

How to Build Your Own Golden Gate Bridge

"To begin with the end in mind means to start with a clear understanding of your destination."
— **Stephen R. Covey**

In the 1920s, Joseph Strauss had an idea that most people thought was impossible: a bridge across the Golden Gate in San Francisco Bay. Such a bridge had been imagined and talked about for years and would increase access to the growing city of San Francisco which was, at the time, the largest city primarily accessible by ferry boats in the United States. But the public had always abandoned such notions because of the widespread belief that a bridge simply couldn't be built.

And their skepticism was well-founded.

Notorious for extreme tides, obscuring fog, and powerful undercurrents, the strait of the San Francisco Bay was only to be crossed at one's peril. Constantly battered by ferocious winds and dangerous waves, many people had lost their lives crossing the unpredictable waters. Not to mention the size of the strait! Spanning over two kilometers and with a depth of over three hundred feet at the center of the earthquake-prone channel, the Golden Gate was a formidable obstacle for even the most prepared of engineering projects. Add on top of that opposition from the Department of War, the US Navy, railroads, and several labor unions; the project was simply too big and too difficult to complete.[1]

However, having previously overseen the construction of hundreds of other bridges, Strauss was confident that it wasn't just feasible but affordable too.

With the help of several other engineers, he proposed a bold vision that captured the imagination. Two steel monoliths towering 230 meters in the air would suspend a 2,000-meter roadway hundreds of feet above the water. His ingenious minimalist approach and proposed budget was also significantly more affordable than several other submitted designs. Most strikingly, colored with a vibrant red that would glow in sunsets, and with bold features embodying the Art Deco style, the bridge would not only be a magnificent fixture of public transportation but would also showcase the possibilities of what could be achieved when art and science were forged together.

After years of public campaigning and raising money, Strauss pressed ahead, and the work began in 1933. As the massive construction rose above the Pacific, the scale of the project was breathtaking to all involved. Millions of rivets, nearly 90,000 tons of steel, and 80,000 miles of wire— enough to wrap around the earth three times—were painstakingly assembled. And after four years, the bridge— which many thought was impossible—was opened in May 1937 to a cheering crowd of over 200,000 people. The perilous journey that once cost lives now took little over two minutes by car.[1]

Since the bridge's opening, it has safely carried millions of people across the treacherous strait and greatly impacted the growing San Francisco economy by making (then inaccessible) land available for expanding the metropolitan area. However, the last time I visited the bridge, I noticed something curious. Even though the bridge was built and designed with the purpose of providing safe transportation for commuters across the water, hundreds of millions of people visit the bridge each year not for daily work and life...but to simply look at it and take pictures.

They may walk across it and stop halfway to appreciate the nice views of the city, or they may go to the other side to capture iconic photos with the bridge framing the landscape all around it. While nice views and sprawling vistas are certainly a *perk* that comes from using the bridge, at the end of the day, providing pretty pictures was not the main objective that Joseph Strauss had in mind when he designed the bridge in the first place. And so, despite the achievements of Strauss and countless other workers, most people today use the Golden Gate Bridge for something it wasn't originally designed for.

How does this connect to the Influence Mindset?

Tribes Are Like Bridges: They Always Have A Destination

What if we considered Tribes the exact same way we consider bridges? For example, Tribes, like bridges, have a specific goal, and they are designed to achieve that goal. Whether that's getting a group of people from one place to another, or accomplishing a specific set of tasks, Tribes always have specific destinations in mind as their primary objective. For example:

- Universities are trying to educate, prepare, and send students out in the world to make a difference.
- Graduate programs are trying to prepare and place students in specialized employment opportunities.
- Companies have specific goals they are trying to achieve. Whether that's to produce and sell more widgets, provide a more effective service, or increase shareholder value, they are trying to accomplish a set of well-defined goals.

Whatever the Tribe, there is always a sense of "we are HERE and want to go THERE"—just like a bridge.

The main difference, however, is that unlike the Golden Gate Bridge (which can accommodate thousands of people every day), there is a limit on how many people can be let into the Tribe. There are only so many

" Tribes always have specific destinations in mind. "

spaces in college. There are only so many open positions in a company. And a person looking for help with his broken pipes can only have so many plumbers.

Because there is an overwhelming number of candidates, Decision Makers have to limit how many people they can let onto their "bridge". That's why, in order to simplify and break down "Choice Overload", Decision Makers ask the third question of the Selective Environment: Why this Tribe?

The Third Key Question: Why This Tribe?

So far, in the previous chapters we have covered the first two questions every Decision Maker asks: "What drives you?" and "What are your credentials?" However, after they've figured out your motivation and qualifications, the third main question they will have is, "Why this Tribe?" This question takes several different forms, but they all boil down to the exact same thing: Why do you want to be a part of this group?

Consider the following examples:

- High school students are asked in college applications, "Why do you want to study here?"
- Prospective graduate students are asked, "What are your goals in our program? Why did you apply here?"
- Career seekers are asked in interviews, "Why are you interested in our company? Why do you want to work here?"
- Professionals are often asked by prospective clients, "Why do you work for your current company? How did you end up choosing them?"

Whatever the situation, you can count on hearing these questions. And if Decision Makers don't specifically ask them upfront, you can guarantee they are at least wondering about it in the back of their minds. All of these questions are essentially recycled versions of the exact same thing, "Why this Tribe? Why are you interested in us? Why do you want to come here?"

The question is a fair one.

If Decision Makers have limited resources to share, they want to make sure that you are a good investment. They want to see if your goals align with the goals of the Tribe. And just like the other two main questions in the Selective Environment, your success rises or falls on how well you answer, "Why this tribe?"

The problem is that the Achievement Mindset is completely ineffective in helping people stand out. Because, as we will see, the Achievement Mindset is more focused on enjoying the views and taking pictures than crossing the bridge to the other side.

"Tourist" Answers

If we could divide up all the people who use the Golden Gate Bridge into groups, they would be placed into two buckets: Commuters and tourists. While commuters use the bridge for its intended purpose of transporting people from one side to another, tourists are there to...well... just take pictures and enjoy the views. When it comes to answering the question, "Why this Tribe?", the Achievement Mindset unfortunately uses what I call "tourist" answers that avoid the real purposes of their target organizations. Instead, they focus on secondary things like perks, possibilities, prominence, and prestige.

Why This Tribe?
ACHIEVEMENT MINDSET

Perks

Possibilities

Prominence

Prestige

Consider these examples:

- College applicants talk about the wide selection and possibilities of majors they can choose from at a university.
- Career seekers say they are attracted to a company because of the amazing benefits and perks of the job.
- Sales representatives and entrepreneurs all boast about their current companies because the firms have influential prominence in their respective industries.

No doubt all these perks, possibilities, prominence, and prestige may be true, but they are *secondary* when compared to the main purpose of an organization. That's because colleges, businesses, and institutions (just like bridges) are meant to get people from "here to there." They do not exist to provide perks, possibilities, and prestige to tourists who want to get on the bridge and THEN figure out their purpose. When you are speaking to a Decision Maker who is looking for and wants to work with commuters, your message will be ineffective if you sound like a tourist.

Plus, everyone else is using the Achievement Mindset and saying the same thing. And so your message becomes noise and is ignored.

If when asked, "Why this Tribe?", all you do is speak of *secondary* and less important things like perks, possibilities, prominence, and prestige, your message is likely to fail, and your chances of success will decrease.

How does the Influence Mindset answer this question differently from the Achievement Mindset?

By proposing Purposeful Partnerships.

Purposeful Partnerships

I once met with a student and their family who was visiting our campus and had questions about admissions. They were from a rural area, and visiting our university was an eye-opening experience. When I asked why she was interested in attending our school, she gave the following response:

"I want to come to this university because I think I will love your campus culture! I like being near people with similar values, but I also enjoy meeting people from around the world. I think this campus would be a great place to experience both of those things. I also look forward to the outdoor lifestyle. I like being outdoors and would want to take a skiing class in the winter. Plus, I bet there is amazing hiking nearby! But probably the biggest reason of all; I've never been to a real college football game and can't wait to cheer for the team in the stadium!"

Campus culture? Outdoor lifestyle? College football games? Over the course of meeting with thousands of students and their families, I probably heard these exact same reasons repeated hundreds of times. Regardless of where they were from or what their socio-economic status was, students from all walks of life gave similar answers. And to be fair, they are perfectly sincere reasons for wanting to come to college. But at the end of the day, if colleges exist to help students successfully step into careers and solve real-world problems, skiing classes and football games are "perks" and benefits. Her response, enthusiastic as it was, was a "tourist" response because she didn't know why she wanted to cross the bridge. She wanted to enjoy the view first.

Let's compare her response to that of another student I was privileged to meet. He was bright, had successfully completed some credit hours at another institution, and was looking to apply as a transfer student. What I didn't know was that he was about to forever change how I looked at the question, "Why this Tribe?"

"I don't know about you," he started, "but my childhood covered about as diverse of backgrounds as was physically possible."

"Really? How so?" I asked.

"My mother is Jamaican and my father is Canadian, and I spent significant time in both countries growing up."

"That must have been a really unique childhood..." I said with curiosity.

"It was," he continued, "and it's because of that unique background that I'm particularly interested in studying here one day."

Intrigued, I invited him to continue. I was looking forward to hearing his perspective.

"Growing up in Jamaica was amazing. I was surrounded by close relatives and had access to gorgeous beaches that were only a stone's throw away. Plus, as you can imagine, there was the most amazing fresh fruit everywhere you could turn. But being in the Caribbean near the beach has its drawbacks. In 1988, we were hit head-on with Hurricane Gilbert, and it devastated our village. Across the island, power was out, flimsy homes were ripped through like cardboard, and we didn't have access to food and clean water."

"That sounds horrible!" I exclaimed.

"It was. But the thing is, despite all the years that people have lived in the direct paths of hurricanes, the Jamaican government was completely unprepared to handle the emergency response. And as a result, people died, and the recovery took even longer. After Hurricane Gilbert, my dad was concerned for our safety, so he moved us up to be near his family in Canada.

"Now, you've probably never heard of Yellowknife," he added, "but it is so far north, it nearly borders the Arctic Circle. In the brief summer, the roads are clear. But in winter? The only way in and out is by modified bush planes. And if there is a storm and something happens, you have to wait a few days before a plane can even get there. The difference is that the people in Yellowknife were prepared for disasters. We all had back-up supplies, we all learned basic first aid in schools, and even though we had intense, and dangerous storms, we rarely had any problems. And that is partly why I am really interested in your university."

Curious, I asked, "How so? Do we have some program connected to Yellowknife?"

"No, but you do have a public health major where I can take classes on emergency response and emergency management. Eventually, I want to work my way to become a county emergency response director and help communities prepare for and withstand natural disasters. Not many universities offer the same kind of course opportunities, but yours does. Plus, being here would allow me to work with the local search and rescue teams and develop a network to make a difference on a national level."

And then he said the word that would forever change my perspective.

"So, in some ways, you could say I am proposing a **partnership** of sorts with your university. I want to go and help communities better handle natural disasters, and you have the exact program and location I need to build a network and career."

I don't know about you, but I was floored.

He wasn't interested in *secondary* things like football games, outdoor lifestyles, and campus life. He wasn't interested in perks, possibilities, prominence, or prestige. Rather, he knew exactly what he wanted to do. He had a goal with a specific destination in mind, and we had a bridge with resources. Together, we were going to help him get from HERE to THERE. He wasn't a "tourist" looking for pictures, but a "commuter" looking for a destination.

He was proposing a purposeful partnership.

Why This Tribe?

ACHIEVEMENT MINDSET	INFLUENCE MINDSET
Perks	
Possibilities	Purposeful Partnerships
Prominence	
Prestige	

Now let me ask you: If you had the choice to accept one student, and you were presented with both examples above, who would you pick? The girl interested in football games or the guy who wanted to study to become an emergency response director? Most would say the second, and I would agree. The first example, though sincere and capable, had a tourist response. But the second? He wanted to use our bridge for its intended purpose. His story positioned him to appear like he would make better use of his time at our university and would have a greater impact as an alumni.

Keep in mind; this problem doesn't just affect college applicants. It also applies to every other type of candidate in the Selective Environment. Let's consider more examples of tourist vs Purposeful Partnership answers and see how they make an impact.

Grad School Candidate

I once interviewed a very competent student who was interested in our graduate program. They had a solid professional background, an excellent GMAT score, and a strong GPA. But when I asked the question, "Why are you interested in our program?", he gave tourist answers.

"Compared to other local MBA programs," he said, "you are much more affordable and highly ranked. I also really like the range of electives you offer and feel like I would have the chance to explore a lot of different areas. I'm not quite sure where I intend to land after the MBA and want to study different areas to figure out my career focus."

Affordability? High rankings? Flexible elective options? Though these are very nice and accurate answers, they are tourist responses because they are all about perks, possibilities, and prestige. To a graduate admissions committee, this kind of answer is a massive red flag because instead of seeing us as a bridge from one part of his career to another, he saw our program as a place where he could stroll around, enjoy the views, and take his time exploring career directions.

The problem was that every aspect of our program, from day one of orientation to the last day of graduation, was not designed to help people stare into their navels and contemplate their life direction. No, our program was geared for one thing and one thing only: to help students get job offers and placed in the next step of their career. Every networking event, every resume prep session, and every job fair had the singular goal of accomplishing this task. And our program success, external rankings, and even institutional funding was determined by how well we achieved these aims.

We were a bridge from one point to another, and we wanted students who knew precisely how they planned to cross it. Though his answer was made in earnest, the last thing we needed was a tourist causing a traffic jam right in the middle of our bridge. And so despite his strong qualifications, he was denied.

Compare that response to another applicant who framed her approach like this: "So far in my career I've worked in smaller tech companies doing a variety of roles, but I really want to take my career to the next level and work for a larger tech company. As you know, there are several tech companies that are within minutes of your campus, and I was excited to discover that your program has close relationships with them. Even better, I researched on LinkedIn that you have several alumni who work there. So aside from using the MBA to increase my skill set to accelerate my career, I specifically want to come here because I know you are better positioned than anyone else to help me build relationships with my target companies and connect me with alumni who work there."

This applicant had specific companies in mind, had clear goals of what she wanted to do, and knew exactly why she wanted to attend our program. She knew our capabilities and was prepared to cross the bridge. Her Influence Mindset approach set her apart.

Who do you think had a message that was more effective? The "affordability and flexible elective options" guy, or the gal who wanted to leverage our alumni network to build relationships with specific companies and further her career? More importantly, if you had to choose one, who would you be more influenced to choose? The Achievement or Influence Mindset candidate?

Career Seekers

When I ran internship programs for an international firm, I interviewed a group of candidates who wanted to land a position at our company. While the interview covered a variety of topics, when asked, "Why do you want to work here?" the majority used tourist responses of prominence, prestige, and possibilities.

One said, "I want to work for this company because it is a leader in global markets!" (He focused on prominence.)

Another said, "I am attracted to come here because you have locations in most countries and have one of the most well-known brands in the world. Plus, your products are extremely popular, and I want to be able to work on one of these existing product lines." (This candidate was focused on prestige as well as prominence.)

A third mentioned, "I really want to come here because this company is very large, and there are a lot of different departments that I could potentially work for." (He lacked direction and instead focused on the range of possibilities our company offered.)

While these were very qualified and capable candidates, it turns out their messaging was all the same because (like the previous examples) they were giving tourist answers. None of them mentioned the core purpose of the company. None of them focused on the strategic corporate goals, or the problems we were trying to solve. None of them talked about wanting to cross "the bridge" we were trying to cross ourselves, but rather they wanted to be in the company simply to admire the view...and then figure out their goals after a while.

Compare their responses to another applicant who said, "One of the most important emerging technologies in the world right now is the 'Internet of Things' (IoT), where all parts of homes and appliances can be connected together and controlled through a single network. I think this is hugely important and has large implications. But not many companies are positioned to do anything about it because of how large of a challenge it is. Your company, however, is positioned to take action. Though there are many reasons I'm interested in working here, I really want to be in a place where I can learn as much as I can about the IoT and find other ways we can safely develop and apply this technology. And I think your company is best positioned to do that."

This last candidate completely stood out from the rest because instead of highlighting perks, prominence, and prestige, he was framing his goal around a purposeful partnership to take advantage of a compelling opportunity. Again, if you had to choose one, who would you be more influenced to choose? Who seems like a more desirable addition to the Tribe? The candidates with the Achievement Mindset answers or the one with the Influence Mindset?

The Influence Mindset stands out again and again.

Sales Professionals

If you are a sales professional who relies on their personal brand and positioning to win clients, this problem applies to you as well. However, it often happens in a different way. Instead of asking, "Why this Tribe?" or, "Why do you want to do business with me?", Decision Makers in the Selective Environment often ask, "Why do you choose to stay with your Tribe?" Or in other words, "Why do you choose to still work for your company?"

Consider these two examples:

I was once speaking with a financial advisor, and as our conversation drew to a close, I asked him, "So of all the financial companies out there, how did you end up choosing this one?"

His response? Tourist answers: "I chose this company because this is a fabulous place to work. The benefits are amazing, the people are great, and the company really takes care of its employees. They do a great job helping with work life balance, and I can tell they really invest in their people. It's a great organization."

His answer was all about the perks and benefits that come from working at the company. Again, there is nothing wrong with that kind of answer, but it fails to influence me. He is basically saying that his company is preferable because it is the equivalent of smart, capable, qualified, and passionate. The problem is that most other companies are also good places to work, and that doesn't really concern me or the problems I need help fixing.

What does the Influence Mindset and "Purposeful Partnerships" look like in a sales environment?

I was speaking with a friend of mine who had recently started working for a financial advising company and was slowly building his own book of business from scratch. When I asked him the same question as above, "Why did you choose to work for this company?", his response caught my attention.

"You know, I've always wanted to make my profession about helping people feel prepared for challenges and have peace of mind about their financial decisions. And when I was looking around at the different companies I could work for, none of them felt right. Either their business models were fundamentally designed to take advantage of clients, or their compensation schemes incentivized me to sell things that my clients really didn't need. But when I looked at this company, I felt like their business model empowered me to help—and not burden—the people I wanted to serve. Sure, I could rattle off numbers about their investment performance and how much money they have under management, but at the end of the day this was the right place for me to work, and I feel empowered to help people in the way that I feel best."

Do you notice the difference?

Instead of building up the perks of the company and speaking of possibilities, prominence, and prestige (like the other example), my friend in the second example instead spoke of how the company was a Purposeful Partnership for his personal mission. And can you see the difference?

When you use Achievement Mindset answers, you are only strengthening the brand of the company. But when you use the Influence Mindset and Purposeful Partnerships, you are simultaneously strengthening your personal brand as well.

Which is the secret to the Influence Mindset response: People choose to do business with *you* just as much as they choose to do business with *your company.* And the Influence Mindset addresses both: It not only sets your company apart, but it sets you apart as well.

But why? When we speak about college applications, job interviews, and sales pitches, how come Purposeful Partnerships seem to stand out so much more effectively than perks, possibilities, prominence, and prestige? Why is it more influential? As it turns out, there are some powerful things happening in the brain when we frame our message around Purposeful Partnerships.

Specifically, it positions you as a strategic thinker and signals you are destined to be part of the Tribe.

Thinking Ahead Sets You Apart

When you communicate in terms of Purposeful Partnerships, not only are people more likely to pay attention to you (because the response is such a novel approach), but more importantly, it signals that you are a strategic thinker.

And you want to be seen as a strategic thinker.

In one study conducted in 2013, researchers found that being a strategic thinker was one of the most powerful ways to be seen as an effective leader. In fact, being perceived as a strategic thinker was twice as important as having strong communication abilities, and almost 50 times more effective than merely being highly skilled.[2]

"People choose to do business with *you* just as much as they choose to do business with *your company*."

I find this highly relevant.

Because while the Achievement Mindset is all about showing how skilled, capable, and qualified someone is, the truth is that this is NOT an effective way to influence others. Showing that you have strategic thinking capabilities through Purposeful Partnerships is far more influential than showcasing a wide variety of skills.

Fifty times more effective, in fact.

However, the most important finding from the study was that people with strategic thinking skills were "four times more likely to be seen as individuals with significant future potential within their organizations."[2] That is an incredibly important finding! While everyone else in the Achievement Mindset is only trying to prove their short-term value to the Tribe, those with the Influence Mindset are framing their candidacy in terms of both short-term AND long-term value. And if Decision Makers have limited spots to award and are trying to decide who to choose, the more you can position yourself both as a short-term and long-term "win", the more likely you are to be successful. Framing your message around Purposeful Partnerships does exactly that.

Proving you have strategic thinking skills positions you as a future asset to the company, and it also sets you apart as a potential leader. As I've mentioned previously, leadership is not the ability to solve problems but rather the ability to identify problems that no one else can see. Study after study has found that strategic thinking is one of the key attributes of effective leaders.[3] So when you speak in terms of Purposeful Partnerships, you signal the ability to think strategically and have another avenue to show others that you have leadership potential.

But the advantages of Purposeful Partnerships don't end there. When you signal that your goals align with the Tribe, you are also showing that you are a part of what researchers call the "In-Group".

"Being perceived as a strategic thinker is almost 50 times more effective than merely being highly skilled."

Fit...Not The Fittest

I once spoke with the president of a real-estate company who shared one of his biggest frustrations in hiring employees.

"Look," he said, "We get all these applicants who have the credentials, have studied in college how to run Excel sheets, and can amaze us with their stories and lofty words. But the problem is that barely any of them know anything about our company. They've seen the job posting...and rather than applying to our company and our team, they only apply to... the job posting. We often get generic resumes, and when they interview, all they do is rattle off facts about themselves. Impressive as they may be, they haven't done any research on us and can't tell why we are different."

He continued with this insightful point: "However, if one of them knew our mission and goals? Then we would know it's a good fit. That would tell us they were interested enough to do the extra research beyond just responding to a job posting, and they would be the right person for our team. It's when people share our vision...not just prove they can do the job...that really catches our interest. That's how we know they are the right people for our team."

Notice what he didn't say.

He didn't say that people with the highest qualifications are the ones chosen. No, he said that when everyone else has similar skill sets, it's the people who share the same vision as the company that are most likely to get hired. What makes people stand out isn't their abilities, but whether or not they "fit" with the Tribe. And when we prefer people who are similar to us, this is what behavioral psychologists call "In-Group Bias."[4]

People are really good at distinguishing between "us" and "them" and forming different kinds of Tribes in nearly every part of life. This happens in situations where race, socio-economic backgrounds, skills, accents, belief systems, and a hundred other types of distinguishing characteristics become apparent. If you and I share some commonality, we might see each other as part of an "In-Group". If we have noticeable differences? Then we would label each other as being different or part of the "Out-Group".

And when it comes to the Selective Environment, you want to be seen as part of the "In-Group".

In-Group Bias

"In-Group Bias" means that we are wired to think that people similar to us are fundamentally...better. Research has shown that we see people in our In-Group as being more intelligent, more moral, and overall better people than those whom we label as part of an Out-Group.[5,6,7] That means we are more likely to give them the benefit of the doubt, have empathy for them, and consider them with less critical eyes. And the opposite is true as well. We are likely to have a bias *against* people who we think are different from us and part of an Out-Group.

If colleges and companies have a unifying commitment to a specific purpose, they are a Tribe. However, when you use Achievement Mindset language and speak of perks, possibilities, etc., you are using language that is completely different from their Tribe's fundamental purpose.

- Colleges don't exist to provide prestige.
- Companies don't exist to provide a wide range of possibilities.
- Start-ups don't exist to provide perks.

No, like a bridge, these entities have a clear goal of getting from "here to there." And when you use Achievement Mindset language, you are speaking of things that are "outside" the goals of the Tribe. Perks, possibilities, and prestige signal that you are part of the Out-Group. And we are wired to be biased against people we see as part of the Out-Group regardless of qualifications.

Hence, the Achievement Mindset and "tourist" answers trigger an unconscious bias against your candidacy and limits your chances of success in the Selective Environment.

However, when you speak in terms of Purposeful Partnerships, you are speaking the language of the Tribe. You are signaling that you share the same values as they do and indicating that you will fit in better with their team. You are positioning yourself to be part of the In-Group and triggering the positive effects of In-Group Bias in your favor.

And when you do this, Decision Makers:

- Are more likely to feel empathy towards you
- Will give you the benefit of the doubt
- Will be less critical of your weaknesses.

In short, using the Influence Mindset and framing your intentions around Purposeful Partnerships will help your message stand out from the crowd and naturally influence Decision Makers to choose you over others.

Wrap-up

In the past few chapters, we have covered how to answer the three main questions Decision Makers ask in a way that captures attention, establishes credibility, and cultivates influence. You have learned how to craft your message so it is designed to bypass the brain's defenses and stand out from the crowd.

You have learned the secrets of the Influence Mindset.

The question now is, how do you put this into action? How do you begin to apply these principles?

In the next section, we cover how to take your next step.

Summary

- When talking about why people want to join a university, a company, or another kind of Tribe, the Achievement Mindset focuses on perks, possibilities, prominence, and prestige.
- But these are ineffective because organizations do not exist to provide these benefits and perks.
- The Influence Mindset frames their goals around Purposeful Partnerships.
- This signals that you are a strategic thinker and are 50 times more likely to influence others to perceive you as a valuable leader.
- It also signals you are part of their In-Group and influences them to consider you more favorably.

Bonus

For more details and exercises on this chapter head over to: **TheChristianHansen.com/BookBonus**

Situation:	PERFORMANCE ENVIRONMENT	SELECTIVE ENVIRONMENT
Definition:	Success is based on how well you perform	Success is based on influencing people to choose you
Primary Goal:	Prove you are smart, capable, qualified, and passionate	Influence someone to choose you over others
Strategy:	Achievement Mindset	Influence Mindset
What Drives You?	Passion	Problem Focused Passion
What Are Your Credentials?	Previous experience, performance indicators, prestige, and percentages	People Centered Problems ↓ People Based Results
Why This Tribe?	Perks, possibilities, prominence, and prestige	Purposeful Partnerships
?	?	?
?	?	?

SECTION 3:

THE FUNDAMENTALS

The Small Man Who Towered Over Kareem Abdul-Jabbar

"If you don't have time to do it right,
when will you have time to do it over?"
—John Wooden

In 1948 when John Wooden took over UCLA's struggling basketball program, few could have imagined that he would become one of the greatest coaches of all time. By the time he retired in 1975, he had led the Bruins to 10 National Championships within the space of 12 years and launched the careers of a generation of NBA stars like Kareem Abdul-Jabbar. Considering Wooden's staggering success, many have wondered how he did it.

One of the answers was his unflinching commitment to the fundamentals of the game of basketball. He tirelessly worked on establishing consistent habits of success that focused on the foundational principles. And this commitment to the basics was no more evident than on the first day of practice of each season. Each year would start the same: teaching his players how to tie their shoes.[1]

Imagine this five-foot-ten man, dwarfed by towering athletes, teaching a skill so mindless, so basic, and so simple as tying a shoe. These young men had played all their lives and knew the game in and out, but each year started the same: learning fundamentals from the bottom up.

The process was undeviatingly formulaic.

First came the socks. As Wooden showed how socks needed to be pulled tight, he stressed that special attention needed to be given to smoothing out wrinkles around the heels and the little toes.

Second came the shoes. Making sure that the laces were loose from top to bottom and the flaps pulled wide, he then showed how you would raise your perfectly socked foot and insert it into the shoe.

Third came the laces. Beginning at the bottom, each lace was tightened through each eyelet until the shoe was snugly fit in place and the maximum amount of lace was ready for tying.

Last came the knot. Using the excess lace now pulled tight, each knot was tied in a double knot.

Each year, the lesson was the exact same. No changes; no alterations.

It begs the question: Why all the focus on shoes? Why go into such detail about mundane things like socks, laces, and knots?

The results speak for themselves.

Wooden knew that basketball is played on a hard floor and the players' feet take a pounding each game. Smooth socks meant players had no blisters, and no blisters meant that few athletes were sidelined due to unnecessary injuries.

With quick sprinting all the time, a split-second reaction could mean the difference between winning and losing. Making sure that the shoes are open and loose before inserting your foot means your foot is getting the maximum surface area within the shoe. Maximum surface area leads to better traction, and better traction cuts reaction time, thus helping players make it across the court.

Wooden also knew that the ankle is one of the most critical joints in the body. Sure, you could get around with a sore elbow or maybe a slightly injured shoulder, but if an ankle is injured? That player is benched. Tight laces pulled through each eyelet means that the ankle gets optimal support from the shoe, and the player reduces the risk of injury.

Lastly, in basketball, time is everything. And if you are delayed for any reason, your opponents have the opportunity to exploit weakness. Ensuring each shoe is tied with a double knot decreases its chance of coming undone and slowing you down in the middle of a game.

Of course there are many other secrets to Coach Wooden's legacy, but the consistent habit of properly putting on a shoe was undoubtedly critical to his players' success.

What are the simple habits that help you execute the Influence Mindset?

In the next chapter, we are going to go over several practices that will increase your ability to influence others. The more you apply them, the more you will stand out.

And the best part is that anyone can learn and practice these skills.

CHAPTER 6

Your Game Plan

"Give me six hours to chop down a tree and
I will spend the first four sharpening the axe."
—**Abraham Lincoln**

Nothing is more humiliating to a ten-year-old than hearing the words, "Strike three! Yeeeeerrrrrrr out!"

And that's exactly what the umpire had just said.

You see, even though it was only my elementary school's field on a Saturday morning, and even though the only people in the stands were a handful of yawning parents in sunglasses, in my mind, this was the biggest baseball game in the world. The match had been a grind. We were pitted against another group of fourth graders from a school across town, and the game lurched slowly through each inning. We were locked in a struggle of such epic proportions that only ten-year-olds could fully grasp the weight of the moment.

This was my second time at bat, and I walked towards the plate with as much swagger as humanly possible. Wearing my lucky sock and furiously chewing my pink bubble gum, I swung my bat several times and stretched my arms, loosening up for the big moment. I felt like a prized thoroughbred primed and ready to tear through a race track and eat everyone else for lunch. Setting my stance, I glared at the pitcher with as much venom and fury that I could muster.

Truth be told, I was actually wildly terrified. My strut, swing, and stare were all for show.

This pitcher was an ace. He was hands down the best fourth-grade pitcher that our town had produced in years, and rumor around the playground was that the kid was being scouted by the LA Dodgers. And we, cross our hearts and hope to die, believed it. He had handily wiped out our entire line-up without even breaking a sweat, and one kid on our team (whose dad worked for NASA) swore the baseballs this pitcher used had secret space technology that broke the fundamental laws of Newtonian physics.

None of us could disagree.

And so, despite my strut and show, I doubted that I had any chance to live. The truth was that I frankly wasn't all that good at baseball. I was an OK batter, but running and catching fly balls were not exactly my strong points. Plus, as I stared down this menace on the mound, my baseball jersey felt extra itchy all of a sudden, my mouth guard made my breathing sound like a Dolby surround sound system, and my oversized helmet smelled like every other kid on my team who had also just worn it. I raised my bat and watched the pitcher go into his windup...

Pffft, Whap!

"Steeeeeee-rike one!" the umpire called.

Wait, that was a pitch? The ball had left his fingers and, like an alien UFO, hovered millimeters above the ground at warp speed. Then at the last second, it seemed to have a mind of its own as it leapt upwards, through the strike zone and into the catcher's glove. I had flinched, wanting to swing, but knew I couldn't hit it.

I was a goner.

Cheers came from the stands as I adjusted my stance and prepped for another.

Pffft, Whap!

"Steeeeeee-rike two!" the umpire called.

I shook my head and blinked in amazement. That ball had come in so fast, I swear it shredded the fabric of time and space itself. The catcher shook his hand to ease the pain and threw the ball back to the pitcher, who leaned forward again, his eyes piercing my soul.

Again, I refocused and did my best to stare him down. This time as he went into his line-up, I leaned into my swing. As the ball came rocketing straight towards me, I swung with all my might. In that moment, despite my face being contorted in concentration, I watched as that ball came and I swear—using voodoo magic that not even my lucky sock could stop— the ball moved midair to avoid my bat.

"Strike three! Yeeeeerrrrrrr out!"

With my hopes and dreams for baseball stardom in tatters, I began the long walk of shame back to the dugout; vanquished. The next member of my team trembled as he grabbed his bat and walked towards his fate. Home plate was quickly becoming a dissection table.

I sat down in defeat. We were doomed and had no chance. It was then that Coach lumbered over and sat next to me saying, "I wanna show you something. Do you know how to read a pitcher?"

"What does that mean?" I asked.

"It means, if you watch their body in the windup, you can tell what kind of pitch they are gonna throw."

Stunned, I said, "You can read a pitcher?"

"Oh sure," he said pointing towards the mound, "This kid they have up there is like the Sunday paper. Watch his legs and his shoulders. When he tilts to the left in the windup, he's gonna throw a curveball. When he tilts to the right, it's gonna be a slider. And then when he leans forward a bit more, just like he's doing now, he is putting his weight into it, and it's gonna be a fastball straight down the middle."

Sure enough, the next pitch shot through the air like a laser and evaded my friend's bat. I could have sworn I saw burn marks and hints of smoke coming from the catcher's glove. But it happened just like Coach said it would! I had fireworks going off in my brain.

"You're telling me he does this every time?"

"Yeah, every time. Each pitcher is different," he added, "but once you watch him; after a while, you can figure out how he does it. He's only got a couple tricks up his sleeve, and once you see his pattern, you can be ready."

From then on, I watched the pitcher like a hawk. And just like Coach said, it was like clockwork. When he began the windup leaning left? Curveball. Tilting right? Slider. Leaning forward? Fast ball down the middle.

I felt as if I had broken the code to the biggest secret in the universe, and I couldn't wait for my next time at bat. When my turn came the next inning, I felt much more ready. This time I walked to home plate with real swagger.

Confused at my different attitude, the pitcher eyed me suspiciously, rolling the ball in his hands. I took my stance at the plate, gripped my bat and waited. I stared at him with nervous anticipation. The windup began, and...he leaned left.

Curveball!

I quickly shifted my weight and swung, and hit! The ball veered right, flying over the dugout, and was a foul ball...but at least I had hit it! I stared at my bat in amazement. I had actually hit the ball!

With renewed confidence, I repositioned myself and watched. The pitcher lifted his leg to create momentum and...tilted right.

Slider!

I extended the bat to right where I knew the ball would be, and again, a hit! This time it shot to the left and over the other dugout. Another foul ball, but a hit nonetheless.

It was working! I was at least hitting the ball! And better yet, I knew EXACTLY what was coming next. With his curveball done and the slider out of the way, all he had left was his fastball...right down the middle. And sure enough, he leaned forward as he began his windup.

I stepped into my swing and felt the amazing feeling of hard Louisville maple wood connecting to the ball; this time a line drive out to right field.

Stunned it had actually worked, I took a moment to realize I needed to run for the base. As I tore past our dugout, I could see coach whooping and hollering with his ball cap in his hand.

By the time I made it to first base, the right fielder had gotten the ball and was ready to throw me out if I dared go for second base. And so I stayed.

I couldn't believe I had actually made it on base. It wasn't a home run, but after a day of strikeouts it sure felt good to get a base hit. More importantly, I had learned how to break the secret code that had levelled our team one by one. And I couldn't wait to try it out again and again.

The Selective Environment Is Like Baseball

Most people enter the Selective Environment just like the first time I walked up to bat. They may appear confident, but they are secretly nervous because they have no idea what's going to happen. When the windup begins and the questions start coming, most people swing blindly, hoping to hit the ball. And, like me, most people miss.

That's because the Achievement Mindset is all about reacting. Instead of taking command of the situation, it conforms and bends entirely to the wishes and intentions of Decision Makers. Essentially, the Achievement Mindset is all about fulfilling the requirements someone else sets. When they ask a question? You give a response. They ask for this piece of information? You deliver it. They say jump and you ask, "How high?"

Pitch here, swing there.

The problem is that when your entire game plan is simply reacting, you give up all your control to Decision Makers. And when people feel as if they have zero control in a high-stakes situation, they get nervous and start making dumb mistakes that ruin their chances.

They swing with all their might and miss every time.

One time I was interviewing a candidate for an MBA program. On paper, he had every reason to be confident. He had solid experience,

"When your entire game plan is simply reacting, you give up all your control."

excellent grades, and I was genuinely looking forward to meeting him. However, the moment he walked into my office, it was clear that he was a bundle of nerves. He was extremely anxious, and despite my best efforts to be welcoming and friendly, he struggled immensely. When I asked basic questions, he seemed completely surprised. When I invited him to help me understand aspects of his resume, he panicked. As the interview went on, he was so nervous that he started to perspire even though the room was a comfortable cool temperature.

Eventually, he asked if he could use the restroom, and of course I said yes. He got up, went down the hall, and instead of using the restroom, he left the building entirely. He was so uncomfortable that he left our interview never to return. But he had left his bag of personal items...with his car keys...inside my office. After about 20 minutes when we figured out he had gone, I gave the bag to our office manager in case he returned.

Sure enough, realizing he couldn't drive out the parking lot, he came back to our office (avoiding me), grabbed his bag, and left.

Now, this is obviously a tragic example, and most people don't usually run out of interviews in tears. But rather than focusing on what this student did, I want us to focus on what *he felt,* because these kinds of emotions impact everyone in the Selective Environment. When the stakes are high and we don't have control, we feel anxious and sometimes afraid. And when your success depends upon delivering your message with confidence, you don't want to feel fear.

What's The Game Plan?
ACHIEVEMENT MINDSET
React Better Than Everyone Else

This Is Your Brain on Fear

Your brain has two competing areas that are in a constant struggle for control. On the one hand, you have the rational part of your brain that focuses on reason, thinking, making intelligent decisions, and so on. On the other hand, you have the survival part of your brain that is wired to recognize threats and keep you alive. While they are always working, only one can be in control at any given time. And so, as you go about your daily life, your brain is constantly evaluating the risks and opportunities around you, hopping back and forth between "rational" mode and "survival" mode.[1]

Most of us whose lives revolve around school, work, friends, and family usually don't find ourselves under constant threat of imminent danger or death. And so for the most part, the "rational" part of our brain tends to be in control. We think, we process, we communicate ideas, and we accomplish complex tasks.

However, let's say you are on a walk and a dog jumps at you. Or, you are driving down a busy road and the car in front of you slams on its brakes. In these situations, you have a split second to react. Just like when you're in a stress-filled situation where your opportunities hang in the balance and your success depends on getting Decision Makers to choose you over everyone else.

Now, you are in a survival situation, and the survival part of your brain takes over.

For the past several million years, our brains have learned to survive by physically evading or fighting off something that was bigger, faster, or stronger. And so, the moment our brain senses a threat or feels fear, it triggers a series of physical reactions that are designed to help you fight or run away.

This is called the fight or flight response.[2]

In a fraction of a second, some amazing things begin to happen throughout your body as your brain is preparing to fight or flee. Instantly, your brain releases stress hormones like cortisol and adrenaline, sending warning signals throughout your body to prepare for immediate action. Your breathing intensifies, your heart rate increases, and blood is diverted from less important organs to your arms and legs in preparation for fending off an attack. Your pupils dilate so you can see more clearly and notice movement better; all details critical for your survival.

As your body is ramping up for war, all this occurs at the expense of one crucial thing: your "rational" brain. As energy is diverted towards survival, your ability to use logic and think reasoned thoughts decreases. Think about it: In stressful situations, have you ever felt your brain become foggy all of a sudden? Sure, you may have noticed unique sounds and remembered small details. But did you struggle to think clearly? Or maybe you felt paralyzed and, despite your best efforts, struggled to speak normal sentences. That's right, as your body was preparing for battle, your rational brain was effectively being hijacked.[3]

That's when we start to make dumb mistakes that ruin our chances in the Selective Environment.

And not even your lucky sock can help.

Consider these examples:

- When writing college essays, most students read the questions and aren't sure what to write, let alone how to write it. They begin to feel anxious, stressed, and afraid, and they agonize over where to even begin. And because college application writing is such a painful and stressful process, many procrastinate and end up submitting essays that completely fail to stand out.

- Job seekers leave interviews kicking themselves because, in the moment, they "froze up" and stumbled on difficult questions. Many feel so nervous that they struggle to sound intelligent and even make costly slip ups. For example, they forgot to mention "that" story or failed to give "that" example that would have made all the difference. Or maybe they missed easy opportunities to build rapport with the interviewer, which could have helped.

- Professionals lose sales opportunities because they miss chances to connect with their prospects. Whether they are standing in front of groups of people, have to cold call, or even make connections at networking events, sometimes sales reps let their nerves get the best of them and they fumble on important opportunities.

In each of these situations in the Selective Environment, the candidates are experiencing some form of the fight or flight response. And despite their best efforts, millions of years of neuro programming is getting in the way of their success. They keep swinging but are more and more likely to miss.

There is, however, some good news.

In the Selective Environment, your survival brain doesn't have to reign supreme. In fact, with a little training and practice, you can ensure that your rational brain remains in control. And instead of tripping up, you can actually thrive.

That's because you can create a game plan. You can know, in advance, the kinds of questions coming your way, and avoid the disastrous effects of the fight or flight response. You can prepare to swing and hit every time. Instead of being reactive, you can predict what is coming and proactively take control in your favor.

This is where the Influence Mindset ties everything we have learned so far together.

It's Time to Read The Pitcher

When I figured out the pitcher only had three tricks up his sleeve, it completely changed how I approached the game. I could tell when each pitch was coming and could then also reasonably guess what was next.

The same thing can happen in the Selective Environment. We all know that there are essentially three main questions that Decision Makers want answered:

- What drives you?
- What are your credentials?
- Why this Tribe?

That's it. Every important piece of information they want to know is connected to these three core questions in some way. Sure, Decision Makers may have other questions that explore other details. Yes, they may ask for specific examples of different things. But at the end of the day, these key points shape and determine the majority of questions in the Selective Environment.

Our challenge is this: Now that you know the "Pitcher's Secret", what are you going to do about it?

Are you going to just walk in (the Achievement Mindset) and hope for the best? Are you only thinking about how to react better than everyone else?

" You can predict what is coming and proactively take control in your favor. "

Or are you going to create a game plan, prepare to notice what types of questions are coming your way, and improve your chances of success?

Let's start making your game plan.

Questions Are Platforms for Influence

While the Achievement Mindset's goal is simply to react better than everyone else, the Influence Mindset is all about looking for opportunities to cultivate influence and stand out. And you will stand out when you focus on framing your message around:

- Problem Focused Passions
- People Centered Problems → People Based Results
- Purposeful Partnerships

"Wait a minute," I can hear you asking, "if they ask a specific question, I can't just ignore it and carry on speaking about People Based Results or Purposeful Partnerships. I have to first answer the question!"

Yes, you are 100% correct.

But the difference is that we need to completely reframe how we look at questions that are asked in the Selective Environment. Instead of seeing a question as something to answer or a concern to resolve, we need to see each question as a platform to pivot and position our message.

What's The Game Plan?

ACHIEVEMENT MINDSET	INFLUENCE MINDSET
React Better Than Everyone Else	Use Each Question as a Platform to Pivot and Position My Message

But how can a question be a platform for your message?

I once read an essay from a student who was asked to write about one of her passions. In the essay, she spoke about her love of music. However, she framed it in this way: "I discovered that while I certainly am passionate about music, I am more passionate about using music as a way to help people. Yes, I enjoyed playing the piano and discovering new ways to interpret complicated passages, but I found I was more interested in seeing how my music helped people find healing. That's why I'm particularly interested in pursuing music therapy, because I see my passion in music as a way to help people recover from debilitating trauma."

Do you notice what she did there? The question basically asked: "What drives you?" And instead of just making her message about passion and music, she pivoted and showed how music *was a tool* to accomplish her Problem Focused Passion.

Another time during a grad school interview, I asked a candidate to explain a particular section of her work history. Instead of just running through the facts and speaking of her performance indicators, she said: "That was a fantastic experience because it taught me how to look at clients in a completely new way. My job was about helping small businesses create and manage their social media marketing campaigns. I was working with one client in particular that seemed difficult at first, but I realized their fears and concerns were because this was their family business and doing a social media campaign meant limiting what their family could eat for the next month. That changed how I approached my work. I realized I was helping people build their lives and invest in their future, not just mechanically and efficiently running campaigns. This changed my approach, and in the end I found better ways to help small businesses make difficult marketing problems easier."

Again, do you see what she did here? I essentially asked, "What are your credentials?" And instead of speaking in terms of performance indicators (like most people), she pivoted and showed how her job *was a tool* to accomplish People Based Results.

She used the question as a platform to pivot and share her message.

Finally, consider this experience I had with a regional sales director from a prominent antique auction house. We happened to be waiting for the same flight in an airport, and I struck up a friendly conversation. After hearing what he did for work, I was fascinated to learn more. When I asked, "So why did you choose to work for this company? Aren't there many similar auction houses out there?" He said, "Yes, there are. But I found that what really gets me up in the morning is helping people get the best value and feel peace of mind when they sell their priceless family treasures."

He continued, "They've put a lot of emotion into these objects, and these things are a deeply personal part of their lives and history. The problem was, when I got to know the other auction houses, they were more concerned with the sale (which is of course, important) but many lacked an institutional culture that really treated people as...people. Which is what I wanted to do. Then, when I found this current company, I noticed that at the forefront, they always focused on the customer and took the extra steps to make sure people had peace of mind when parting with their heirlooms. That's how I knew this is the company I want to match my values with. And the more I've worked there, the more I've found it to be true."

The question I asked was, "Why this Tribe? How did you choose to work with them?" And he illustrated how his purposeful partnership with this company *was a tool* to accomplish his Problem Focused Passion and achieve People Based Results.

In each of these cases, the individuals used the basic questions as platforms to pivot and share their messages and shape the direction of the conversation. They weren't just reacting but were creating opportunities to cultivate influence.

They saw the pitch coming, positioned themselves, and hit the ball with great effect.

And that's exactly what the Influence Mindset does. Instead of just reacting and answering the basic questions, you have a clear destination in mind of where you want the answer to go. True, Decision Makers may set the stage of where to start. However, with the Achievement Mindset, you simply react to Decision Makers, whereas with the Influence Mindset, you see what's ahead, know what question is coming, and use each question as a platform to pivot and determine the destination of each answer.

Wrap-up

I remember receiving the advice, "Make a list of your best stories" so that in interviews, applications, etc. I could be ready to stand out and give the strongest examples possible. I now feel this is ineffective because, like everyone else with the Achievement Mindset, all the other candidates will also have a list of their best stories.

But when you have the Influence Mindset, you first define the main points you want to make. Then, once you have those ideas solidified, you can prepare the best stories that support those points. And if you know, in advance, exactly what kinds of pitches are coming down the line, you can be prepared to pivot and position yourself for success every single time.

Remember: Your goal is to stand out, not merely prove you are outstanding.

And when you walk into the Selective Environment with a clear vision and know exactly how to use the key questions as platforms to pivot and position your message, you will stand out from everyone else who has no clue what pitch is even coming.

"You can be prepared to pivot and position yourself for success every single time."

Summary

- In the Performance Environment, success depends on how well you react.

- But in the Selective Environment, success depends on using the questions as platforms to share your message. And you know the three key questions will be there...every single time.

- You can either use the Achievement Mindset, hope for the best, and experience the fight or flight response, or you can prepare and create a game plan in advance and be much more effective.

- Your goal is to stand out, not just prove you are outstanding.

Bonus

For more details and exercises on this chapter head over to: **TheChristianHansen.com/BookBonus**

Situation:	PERFORMANCE ENVIRONMENT	SELECTIVE ENVIRONMENT
Definition:	Success is based on how well you perform	Success is based on influencing people to choose you
Primary Goal:	Prove you are smart, capable, qualified, and passionate	Influence someone to choose you over others
Strategy:	Achievement Mindset	Influence Mindset
What Drives You?	Passion	Problem Focused Passion
What Are Your Credentials?	Previous experience, performance indicators, prestige, and percentages	People Centered Problems ↓ People Based Results
Why This Tribe?	Perks, possibilities, prominence, and prestige	Purposeful Partnerships
Game Plan:	Reactive	Proactive, predictive
?	?	?

CONCLUSION:

**A STORY
PEOPLE WILL
REMEMBER**

How To Sell Ice Cream in Winter (Even in Vermont)

"If you don't give the market the story to talk about,
they'll define your brand's story for you."
—**David Brier**

"Your brand is what people say about you when
you are not in the room."
—**Jeff Bezos**

In 1980, Ben Cohen and Jerry Greenfield were making one of the biggest business decisions of their lives: Should they continue to sell ice cream by the scoop? Or should they expand and sell it by the pint in grocery stores? Little did they know that this decision was about to impact the lives of millions of people.

A few years earlier in 1977, when they started their ice cream parlor in the college town of Burlington, Vermont, few people could have predicted Ben & Jerry's success. For starters, how do you sell ice cream in a city famous for extremely cold temperatures most of the year? Located on the iconic Lake Champlain, sure, Burlington had warm (yet short) summers. But in winter? Cold fronts would frequently descend from Quebec to the north, and ice-filled nor'easters would invade from the Atlantic to the east. Add to the mix the snow squalls that would unpredictably form over frozen Lake Champlain, and you had a recipe that would make the prospects of any ice cream store...chilling.

But all of this paled in comparison to a more fundamental challenge: Of the two founders, Ben, could neither taste nor smell.[1] That's right, since childhood he had suffered from extreme anosmia, which is also known as "smell blindness", and he had always struggled to enjoy food.

Of the dynamic dessert duo, one of them couldn't even taste what they were selling.

However, both of these challenges (odd location and no sense of smell) proved to be the secrets to their success. While Vermont can be cold, it is also known for excellent dairy. And Ben and Jerry used this to their advantage. In a time when ice cream shops around the country were beginning to experiment with cost-cutting strategies and cheaper additives, Ben and Jerry had easy access to high quality milk, which made their ice cream more enjoyable and affordable.

But it was Ben's struggling taste buds that really made the difference.

While most other premium ice cream brands prided themselves on subtle and refined flavors, Ben and Jerry unabashedly tried a different avenue: texture. Since Ben struggled to taste what they were making, they decided to create flavors that involved huge chunks of added delectables. If he couldn't taste the cookie dough? He simply added more. If he couldn't taste the peanut butter? Then he made the flavors stronger and added more peanut chunks. What resulted was a quirky ice cream packed with flavors and exploding with unique textures.

Oddly enough, the very two obstacles that most thought would ruin their chances ended up producing a premium ice cream that Burlington had never experienced before.

And people loved it.

Business boomed, and Ben & Jerry's gradually expanded until 1980 when they faced the next question: Should they continue focusing on serving ice cream locally by the scoop, or nationally by the pint? On the one hand, they knew the ice cream scoop business well, but it was costly and difficult to expand. However, if they could sell it by the pint? They could reach millions of people.

The problem was that freezer sections across the country were already packed; not just with ice cream, but with the competition. If they were to expand, how could these two guys with their quirky Vermont-grown ice cream flavors stand out when everyone else was trying to stand out too?

The (Really) Cold War

Without a doubt, two of their biggest competitors were Häagen-Dazs and Breyers. Each were massive companies with formidable capabilities, and each had dominated the market for premium grocery store ice cream for years. On the one hand, Häagen-Dazs prided itself on its high-quality ingredients and refined flavors. On the other, Breyers boasted of their prestigious heritage (having been founded in 1860) as well as their simple ingredients.

Sure, Ben and Jerry could go scoop for scoop against Häagen-Dazs on quality, and they could also match Breyer's simple ingredients list. But how could they stand a chance against such established companies?

Their solution? Brilliant branding and marketing.

First it was an attempt at making the world's largest ice cream sundae (weighing in at 27,000 pounds). Then it was driving across the country in the newly invented "cow-mobile" and serving free ice cream everywhere they went. They were even the first ice cream company to create and name a flavor after a rock star, the "Cherry Garcia". They were so successful at getting their name out and creating a completely new brand experience with ice cream, that Häagen-Dazs and their parent company Pillsbury refused to let their distributors sell the Ben & Jerry's brand in Boston.[2]

Naturally, Ben and Jerry saw this as yet another marketing opportunity and went public with the now famous "What's the Doughboy Afraid Of?" campaign, and Häagen-Dazs melted under the pressure.[2]

The Freezer Section Today

Today, Ben & Jerry's ice cream is the most popular ice cream brand in the United States[3] and regularly achieves hundreds of millions of dollars in sales.[4] All this while still producing quirky, texture-filled flavors that people love. One reason for their success was their ability to create a brand-messaging experience that was completely different from every other company out there.

"They created a brand-messaging experience that was completely different from every other company out there.""

And they still do.

The next time you go to a grocery store, spend a little extra time in the ice cream section (go ahead, I give you permission) and just read the labels. What messaging do you see? Chances are you will read the exact same things that Häagen-Dazs and Breyers were saying in the 1980s:

We are high quality

Finest ingredients

Time-honored recipes

Delicious flavors

Creamiest textures

Based on tradition

Passion for excellence.

Do you see a familiar theme?

Even in premium ice cream marketing, the Achievement Mindset is still touting performance, prestige, passion, and qualifications. The problem is, everyone is doing it too.

But then look over the messaging for Ben & Jerry's. If you buy their ice cream, what kind of story are you buying into? How do their flavors make you feel compared to other brands? You will notice they look (and taste) different, have a "who cares?" attitude, and make you want to enjoy them again and again. Even though their annual sales repeatedly reach over half a billion dollars, every time you open a pint of Ben & Jerry's you still feel like you are buying ice cream from two guys in a converted gas station in Burlington, Vermont.

And one of them can't even taste.

Never Has It Been More Important

At its heart, the story of Ben and Jerry captures the full impact of the Influence Mindset. Yes, they had quality ingredients (just like everyone else). And yes, they had delicious flavors (just like everyone else). But more importantly, while every other brand built their messaging around quality and prestige (and got lost in the noise), Ben and Jerry created a message—and ultimately a brand identity—that captured attention, stood out from the crowd, and cultivated influence.

And they didn't rise to the top just because they were quirky (as some people suppose). Instead, they built their success on the three fundamental principles of the Influence Mindset. They were:

- Solving a problem (Ben's struggling taste buds and his need for texture).
- Telling stories about themselves and other people (through creative marketing and innovative flavor names).
- Inviting people to partner with them in a cause (two guys against the ice cream establishment).

And despite entering one of the most competitive markets, they successfully drew people to their brand.

In addition to their flavors, it was their message that made (and continues to make) them truly successful.

Which brings us to you.

Just like Ben and Jerry, your message, and more specifically, your personal brand, is your greatest tool to influence others to choose you. Just as you walk through your local freezer section overwhelmed by the abundance of options, so too are Decision Makers overwhelmed in the Selective Environment.

However, there is hope.

In a world which increasingly prioritizes communication and emotional intelligence, those who can effectively craft and present their message will beat those who can't...every single time. And the truth is that most people don't know how to present, or even have, a compelling personal message.

Never has it been more important to shape people's perceptions about you.

Never has it been more important to stand out from the crowd.

Never has it been more important to have a personal brand intentionally designed to rise above the noise and influence Decision Makers to choose you.

The Real Power of The Influence Mindset

As we reach the end of our discussion, this is my question for you: When a Decision Maker encounters your "brand", what is the story they are buying into? How does your brand make them feel compared to everyone else? More importantly, when people talk about you, what is the brand story you want them to remember and share with others?

"Your message, and more specifically, your personal brand, is your greatest tool to influence others to choose you."

This is exactly where the Influence Mindset comes in. Even though we have discussed your "message", throughout this book, we are really referring to the art and science of crafting a personal brand that reaches the hearts and minds of people and opens the doors of opportunity.

What Is Your Brand Message?

ACHIEVEMENT MINDSET	INFLUENCE MINDSET
Performance, Prestige, Passion, and Qualifications	A Story People Will Remember and Want to Share with Others

With an influential personal brand, you will avoid common obstacles and know what strategies to employ to increase your chances of success.

With an influential personal brand, you will look at common situations differently, identify subtle opportunities that most others miss, and better position yourself for success.

Most importantly, while everyone else has no idea that the game has changed and that the Achievement Mindset utterly fails to make them stand out in the Selective Environment, with an influential personal brand you will stand out from the crowd, rise above the noise, and influence Decision Makers to choose you. And this applies whether you are applying to higher education, searching for your dream job, or even trying to win clients. Because when your personal brand is based on:

- Problem Focused Passions
- People Based Results
- and Purposeful Partnerships

...you will increase your chances of success and provide the foundation for a lifetime of influence.

Perhaps most important of all: As you apply the principles in this book, you will find that the Influence Mindset will bring about an even deeper transformation; not just in how others view you. Because as your personal brand becomes infused with purpose, and as you wield your message to reach your goals, you will ultimately build confidence in... yourself.

And when you have confidence in who you are and in what you can offer the world, that is the greatest influence of all.

SUMMARY TABLE

Situation:	PERFORMANCE ENVIRONMENT	SELECTIVE ENVIRONMENT
Definition:	Success is based on how well you perform	Success is based on influencing people to choose you
Primary Goal:	Prove you are smart, capable, qualified, and passionate	Influence someone to choose you over others
Strategy:	Achievement Mindset	Influence Mindset
What Drives You?	Passion	Problem Focused Passion
What Are Your Credentials?	Previous experience, performance indicators, prestige, and percentages	People Centered Problems ↓ People Based Results
Why This Tribe?	Perks, possibilities, prominence, and prestige	Purposeful Partnerships
Game Plan:	Reactive	Proactive, predictive
Your Brand Message:	Performance, prestige, passion, and qualifications	A story people will remember and want to share with others

Acknowledgements

"It takes a village..." the proverb goes, "to raise a child." While that adage is certainly true for children, I think anyone who has published anything will agree it also takes a village to write a book. Especially, in this case, a book designed to change lives.

True, this book only took a few months to write. But that writing was only possible because of years of observations, conversations, and coaching with more people than I can count. First there were ideas, and then those ideas turned to spoken words. Eventually the words were sketched in notebooks, and then larger concepts gradually took shape on whiteboards and through countless conversations. Then came the research, the stories, endless revisions, and countless drafts...and the book you hold in your hand is the final product.

At the heart of it all, I had a village to help me every step of the way.

First, I would like to acknowledge my mentors and colleagues from my time in higher education. Your commitment to student success and increased access to education is inspirational, and I count myself lucky to have rubbed shoulders with you. Go Cougs and Zot Zot!

Second, I would like to thank my Tribe of dear friends and family who were abundantly willing to let me hash out my thoughts over months of texts, phone calls, and hikes. Not only did they refine and strengthen my ideas, but they also provided critically needed feedback to my manuscript. Despite my best efforts, writing almost always occurs in isolation, and my Tribe always pulled me out of my own head to see the larger picture.

Third, I would like to thank my parents Kathie and John as well as my uncle Bent Hansen. Without their support, love, and encouragement, this book and so much more of who I am would never have been possible. Taking the time to listen, advise, and always add optimistic encouragement helped me believe that my ideas mattered and would work. I love you and am grateful for you.

Fourth, and most important of all, I am grateful for my wife Nathalie and her inexhaustible patience. She has read and kindly listened to more versions of this book than anyone, and her suggestions have been invaluable. Although I ended the book saying confidence is the greatest influence of all, I may have missed the mark because Nathalie has proven time and time again that kindness (more so than any other attribute) is truly the greatest influence of all. I love you.

—Christian Hansen

References

Chapter 2: How The Brain Blocks Noise (And Your Message Too)

1. Bohn, Roger & Short, James. (2009). How Much Information? 2009 Report on American Consumers.

2. Azevedo, Frederico A. C., et al. "Equal Numbers of Neuronal and Nonneuronal Cells Make the Human Brain an Isometrically Scaled-up Primate Brain." *The Journal of Comparative Neurology*, vol. 513, no. 5, 2009, pp. 532–41. *Crossref*, doi:10.1002/cne.21974.

3. Heim, Sabine, and Andreas Keil. "Too Much Information, Too Little Time: How the Brain Separates Important from Unimportant Things in Our Fast-Paced Media World." *Frontiers for Young Minds*, vol. 5, 2017. *Crossref*, doi:10.3389/frym.2017. 00023.

4. New York University. "How the brain separates relevant, irrelevant information." ScienceDaily. ScienceDaily, 20 September 2016. <www.sciencedaily.com/releases/2016/09/ 160920112620.htm>.

5. Haynes, Graeme A. "Testing the Boundaries of the Choice Overload Phenomenon: The Effect of Number of Options and Time Pressure on Decision Difficulty and Satisfaction." *Psychology and Marketing*, vol. 26, no. 3, 2009, pp. 204–12. *Crossref*, doi:10.1002/mar.20269.

6. Iyengar, Sheena & Lepper, Mark. (2001). When Choice is Demotivating: Can One Desire Too Much of a Good Thing? *Journal of personality and social psychology*, 79, 995–1006, *Crossref*, doi:10.1037/0022-3514.79.6.995.

7. Reutskaja, E., Lindner, A., Nagel, R. et al. Choice overload reduces neural signatures of choice set value in dorsal striatum and anterior cingulate cortex. *Nat Hum Behav* 2, 925–935 (2018). https://doi.org/10.1038/s41562-018-0440-2.

8. IESE Business School. "Can't Decide What To Order? Why The Human Brain Struggles With 'Plenty Of Choice.'" *Forbes*, 5 Nov. 2018, www.forbes.com/sites/iese/2018/11/05/cant-decide-what -to-order-why-the-human-brain-struggles-with-plenty-of-choice.

Section 2: The Small Catalog That Made a Big Difference

1. "BBC World Service - 50 Things That Made the Modern Economy, Mail Order Catalogue." *BBC*, 4 May 2019, www.bbc.co.uk/programmes/w3csz2w7.

2. Haldane, Andrew. "The Short Long." 29th Société Universitaire Européene de Recherches Financières Colloquium, Keynote, Brussels, 11 May 2011.

Chapter 3: Why Pursuing Your Passions Is The Worst Idea!

1. Damon, William. *The Path to Purpose: How Young People Find Their Calling in Life*. Reprint, Free Press, 2009.

2. Hurst, Aaron, and Anna Tavis. Imperative, 2015, *2015 Workforce Purpose Index.*

3. Foley, N. C., et al. "Novelty Enhances Visual Salience Independently of Reward in the Parietal Lobe." *Journal of Neuroscience*, vol. 34, no. 23, 2014, pp. 7947–57. *Crossref*, doi:10.1523/jneurosci.4171-13.2014.

4. Costa, Vincent D., et al. "Dopamine Modulates Novelty Seeking Behavior during Decision Making." *Behavioral Neuroscience*, vol. 128, no. 5, 2014, pp. 556–66. *Crossref*, doi:10.1037/a0037128.

5. Johnson, Stefanie K. "I Second That Emotion: Effects of Emotional Contagion and Affect at Work on Leader and Follower Outcomes." *The Leadership Quarterly*, vol. 19, no. 1, 2008, pp. 1–19, *Crossref*, doi:10.1016/j.leaqua.2007.12.001.

6. Hurst, Aaron, and Anna Tavis. Imperative, 2015, *2015 Workforce Purpose Index.*

7. Wang, Yinying. "Pulling at Your Heartstrings: Examining Four Leadership Approaches From the Neuroscience Perspective." *Educational Administration Quarterly*, vol. 55, no. 2, 2018, pp. 328–59. *Crossref*, doi:10.1177/0013161x18799471.

8. Molenberghs, Pascal, et al. "The Neuroscience of Inspirational Leadership: The Importance of Collective-Oriented Language and Shared Group Membership." *Journal of Management*, vol. 43, no. 7, 2015, pp. 2168–94. *Crossref*, doi:10.1177/01492063 14565242.

9. Schjoedt, Uffe, et al. "The Power of Charisma—Perceived Charisma Inhibits the Frontal Executive Network of Believers in Intercessory Prayer." *Social Cognitive and Affective Neuroscience*, vol. 6, no. 1, 2010, pp. 119–27. *Crossref*, doi:10.1093/scan/nsq023.

Chapter 4: How to Avoid Being Average

1. Nelson, K. (2003). Narratives and the Emergence of a Consciousness of Self. In G. D. M. Fireman, T.E.; Flanagan, O.J. (Ed.), Narrative and Consciousness: Literature, Psychology and the Brain (pp. 17-36). New York, NY: Oxford University Press.

2. Loewenstein, G. (2010). Insufficient Emotion: Soul-searching by a Former Indicter of Strong Emotions. Emotion Review, 2(3), 234-239, *Crossref*, doi:10.1177/1754073910362598.

3. Lin, P. Y., Grewal, N. S., Morin, C., Johnson, W. D., & Zak, P. J. (2013). Oxytocin increases the influence of public service advertisements. PLoS One, 8(2), e56934, *Crossref*, doi:10.1371/journal.pone.0056934.

4. Zak, P. J. (2015). Why inspiring stories make us react: the neuroscience of narrative. Cerebrum: the Dana forum on brain science, 2015, 2.

5. Adolphs, Ralph, et al. "The Human Amygdala in Social Judgment." *Nature*, vol. 393, no. 6684, 1998, pp. 470–74. *Crossref*, doi:10.1038/30982.

6. Phelps, Elizabeth A., and Joseph E. LeDoux. "Contributions of the Amygdala to Emotion Processing: From Animal Models to Human Behavior." *Neuron*, vol. 48, no. 2, 2005, pp. 175–87. *Crossref*, doi:10.1016/j.neuron.2005.09.025.

7. Riem, Madelon M. E., et al. "Oxytocin Modulates Amygdala, Insula, and Inferior Frontal Gyrus Responses to Infant Crying: A Randomized Controlled Trial." *Biological Psychiatry*, vol. 70, no. 3, 2011, pp. 291–97. *Crossref*, doi:10.1016/j.biopsych.2011.02.006.

8. Zak, Paul J., et al. "Oxytocin Increases Generosity in Humans." *PLoS ONE*, edited by Sarah Brosnan, vol. 2, no. 11, 2007, p. e1128. *Crossref*, doi:10.1371/journal.pone.0001128.

9. Zak, Paul J. "Why inspiring stories make us react: the neuroscience of narrative." *Cerebrum: the Dana forum on brain science*, vol. 2015, 2, 2 Feb. 2015.

10. Morris, B.S., Chrysochou, P., Christensen, J.D. *et al.* Stories vs. facts: triggering emotion and action-taking on climate change. *Climatic Change* 154, 19–36 (2019).

11. Sobota, Rosanna, et al. "Oxytocin Reduces Amygdala Activity, Increases Social Interactions, and Reduces Anxiety-like Behavior Irrespective of NMDAR Antagonism." *Behavioral Neuroscience*, vol. 129, no. 4, 2015, pp. 389–98. *Crossref*, doi:10.1037/bne0000074.

12. Hurlemann, R., et al. "Oxytocin Enhances Amygdala-Dependent, Socially Reinforced Learning and Emotional Empathy in Humans." *Journal of Neuroscience*, vol. 30, no. 14, 2010, pp. 4999–5007. *Crossref*, doi:10.1523/jneurosci.5538-09.2010.

13. Theodoridou, Angeliki, et al. "Oxytocin and Social Perception: Oxytocin Increases Perceived Facial Trustworthiness and Attractiveness." *Hormones and Behavior*, vol. 56, no. 1, 2009, pp. 128–32. *Crossref*, doi:10.1016/j.yhbeh.2009.03.019.

Chapter 5: How To Build Your Own Golden Gate Bridge

1. Charles River Editors. *The Golden Gate Bridge: The History of San Francisco's Most Famous Bridge*. CreateSpace Independent Publishing Platform, 2015.

2. "Develop Strategic Thinkers Throughout Your Organization." *Harvard Business Review*, 2 Nov. 2014, hbr.org/2014/02/develop-strategic-thinkers-throughout-your-organization.

3. Craig, William. "Strategic Thinkers Are Found to Be the Most Highly Effective Leaders." *Forbes*, 27 Feb. 2018, www.forbes.com/sites/williamcraig/2018/02/27/strategic-thinkers-are-found-to-be-the-most-highly-effective-leaders.

4. "APA Dictionary of Psychology." *Dictionary of Psychology*, dictionary. apa.org/ingroup-bias. Accessed 12 Mar. 2021.

5. Ellemers, N. "The Group Self." *Science*, vol. 336, no. 6083, 2012, pp. 848–52. *Crossref*, doi:10.1126/science.1220987.

6. Culotta, E. "Roots of Racism." *Science*, vol. 336, no. 6083, 2012, pp. 825–27. *Crossref*, doi:10.1126/science.336.6083.825.

7. Everett, Jim A. C., et al. "Preferences and Beliefs in Ingroup Favoritism." *Frontiers in Behavioral Neuroscience*, vol. 9, 2015. *Crossref*, doi:10.3389/fnbeh.2015.00015.

Section 3: The Small Man Who Towered Over Kareem Abdul-Jabbar

1. Vecsey, George. "With Wooden as Teacher, The First Lesson Was Shoelaces." *The New York Times*, 5 June 2010, www.nytimes. com/2010/06/05/sports/ncaabasketball/05wizard.html.

Chapter 6: Your Game Plan

1. Heim, Sabine, and Andreas Keil. "Too Much Information, Too Little Time: How the Brain Separates Important from Unimportant Things in Our Fast-Paced Media World." *Frontiers for Young Minds*, vol. 5, 2017. *Crossref*, doi:10.3389/frym.2017.00023.

2. Saab, Arash The Javanbakht And Linda Conversation. "What Happens in the Brain When We Feel Fear." *Smithsonian Magazine*, 27 Oct. 2017, www.smithsonianmag.com/science-nature/what-happens-brain-feel-fear-180966992.

3. Mohney, Gillian. "The Science of Fear: What Happens to Your Body After a Good Scare." *ABC News*, 1 Nov. 2015, abcnews.go.com/ Health/science-fear-body-good-scare/story?id= 34855202.

Conclusion: How To Sell Ice Cream in Winter (Even in Vermont)

1. "10 Fun Facts About Our Funky Chunks." *https://www.benjerry.com*, 18 Oct. 2018, www.benjerry.com/whats-new/2018/10/chunks-fun-facts.

2. Newsweek Staff. "Cookies, Cream 'N' Controversy." *Newsweek*, 14 Mar. 2010, www.newsweek.com/cookies-cream-n-controversy-194604.

3. "America's 7 Most Popular Ice Cream Brands." *DoDo Cookie Dough & Ice Cream*, 4 July 2019, dodocookiedough.com/popular-ice-cream-brands.

4. Statista. "Sales of the Leading Ice Cream Brands of the U.S. 2020." *Statista*, 11 Feb. 2021, www.statista.com/statistics/190426/top-ice-cream-brands-in-the-united-states.